Illustrator:
Wendy Chang

Editor:
Evan D. Forbes, M.S. Ed.

Editor in Chief:
Sharon Coan, M.S. Ed.

Art Director:
Elayne Roberts

Associate Designer:
Denise Bauer

Production Manager:
Phil Garcia

Imaging:
Alfred Lau
James Edward Grace

Acknowledgements:
Kid Pix®, *Kid Pix 2®*, and *Kid Pix Studio®*, Copyright Brøderbund Software, Inc. 1996. All Rights Reserved.

Publishers:
Rachelle Cracchiolo, M.S. Ed.
Mary Dupuy Smith, M.S. Ed.

Kid Pix ™
for
Terrified Teachers

Authors:

Marsha Lifter, M.A.
and Marian E. Adams

Teacher Created Materials, Inc.
6421 Industry Way
Westminster, CA 92683
www.teachercreated.com

©1997 Teacher Created Materials, Inc.
Reprinted, 1999
Made in U.S.A.

ISBN-1-57690-183-1

Table of Contents

Introduction to Kid Pix

You have obviously made a wise choice in purchasing *Kid Pix*. Every time you use *Kid Pix*, you will be amazed at its capabilities, as well as your own. If you think you have no artistic talent when it comes to drawing on paper, just give *Kid Pix* a try and watch your artistic skills change from stick figures to elaborate works of art.

Empowering children/students to create something using a computer is what using computers at the lower elementary level is all about. For example, once while I was in a lab setting while using *Kid Pix* with a group of six-year-olds, the most wonderful event occurred. The students had been working on their projects for about 45 minutes, when all of a sudden one of the little girls in the class was standing on her chair shouting, "Oh my God, look what I did!" It was at that moment that I realized the importance of computers.

Using *Kid Pix*

This book is intended for classroom teachers who teach children from the third through the fifth grade. Many of the projects can be adapted for use in other grades and in special programs. English Language Development, Special Education, and Gifted and Talented students will find delight in their *Kid Pix* discoveries.

The projects in this book are intended to be used as "task cards" either at a classroom computer station or in a computer lab. Duplicate each project page on a separate piece of tagboard, laminate them, assemble the cards in order, and there you have it, a ready-to-go computer lesson for your students.

The projects are written at a primary level and encompass the different disciplines found in the primary grades. As you become more familiar with *Kid Pix*, you will find a myriad of ways in which to use it in your classroom.

Getting Started with the Kid Pix Program

Kid Pix is available for Macintosh, IBM and compatible PCs, and Windows machines. *Kid Pix Studio* is an enhanced CD-ROM version and is available for both Macintosh and IBM platforms. There is a section in this book dedicated to the additional features of *Kid Pix Studio*. (See pages 92–97.) There is also a walk through *Kid Pix Studio* on pages 98–129.

Discovering the capabilities of *Kid Pix* for yourself will make demonstrating *Kid Pix* to your students much easier; besides, you will have a great time doing it. It will take you less than an hour to begin your foray into the creativity of *Kid Pix*. Use A Walk Through *Kid Pix* on pages 26–64 as a guide to beginning your exploration. The walk-through gives you a feel for the possibilities of what *Kid Pix* can do. When you print your first creation, you will undoubtedly be hooked.

It is very important to demonstrate the basic tools that are used in *Kid Pix* to your class. This can be done with whatever configuration you have in your classroom or lab. Refer to the section on Managing Your Classroom for *Kid Pix* (pages 13–23).

When students first start using *Kid Pix*, it is imperative that they work in an exploration mode. As they discover the various consequences and options of each tool, an air of excitement will build. Students who may not be thought of as popular or talented will gain instant notoriety as they discover new ways of using the *Kid Pix* tools.

You will often hear, "Hey, how did you do that?" while students are working with *Kid Pix*. It will be amazing to watch your students working cooperatively with each other as they complete their *Kid Pix* projects.

Students should have the opportunity to save their work as they create. Most of the projects in this book have two levels: This Project and What Else Can We Do? The first part, This Project, takes each student through the steps to a completed project, and the What Else Can We Do? section extends the project even further. Young computer users might only complete the first section, while more experienced computer users can continue through to the end.

Computers vary as to the method for saving onto a disk or hard drive. It is best to consult your computer manual for saving instructions.

It is best for all students to have their own disks for saving their computer projects. Just the ownership of a disk gives the students a grown-up feeling and a sense of responsibility. Also, as your students move to the next grade, they can take their disks with them. Their disks can become electronic portfolios.

Learning Keyboarding Skills

It will be important that your students have keyboarding skills as they work on their *Kid Pix* projects. This will allow them to work more creatively on the computer, rather than spending their time locating keys and deciding how to use them. On pages eight and nine you will find some ideas for transition-time or sponge activities which build keyboarding skills, as well as reproductions of Macintosh and IBM keyboards for your use.

This Project

With the prevalence of computers in both the classroom and home, there is a definite need for young students to become familiar with the keyboard. As students begin using computers more and more for writing their own stories, they may at times lose their flow of writing while searching for the correct keys. Familiarizing young students with the keyboard will help to alleviate the hunt-and-peck method and lead to a smoother writing activity. To address this need, you will find a graphic of a Macintosh keyboard as well as an IBM keyboard on pages 10 and 11 and some classroom suggestions for keyboarding activities on pages eight and nine.

Before Beginning

- Using a keyboard, demonstrate to your students the correct positions on the home row and how those fingers remain on the home row even when reaching for letters above or below the home row. Have your students color in the home row of keys so they stand out.

- Show your students how the thumb is used to press the space bar.

- Duplicate the keyboard blackline masters found on pages 10 and 11 at an enlargement of 150%. Then you can either laminate them or slip them into plastic sleeves and keep them at students' desks.

Keyboarding Activities

Using one of the keyboards on pages 10 and 11, the following activities can be used as transition-time activities in your classroom—those three minutes before recess and after math, before going to lunch, or even before the end of the day.

- Make a list of the week's spelling words either on the board or on an overhead. Then have your students practice typing each word.

- Have your students practice locating special keys on the keyboard (e.g., tab, space bar, return, shift, delete, etc.).

- Write a math problem on the board and have your students type in the numbers to match the problem.

- Have your students practice writing their friends' names, using the shift key for capital letters.

- Write a letter on the board and have your students find that letter on their keyboards.

- You might want to choose a special word of the day and have your students practice typing it.

- Have your students practice typing holiday names. The capital letters are good practice for using the shift key.

- Write the day and date on the board and have your students type them on their keyboards.

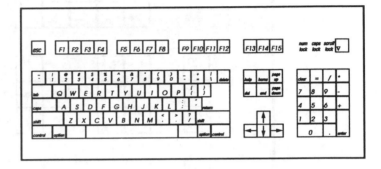

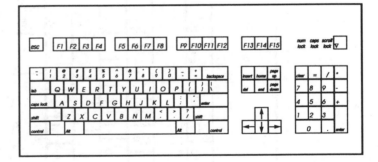

Mac Keyboard

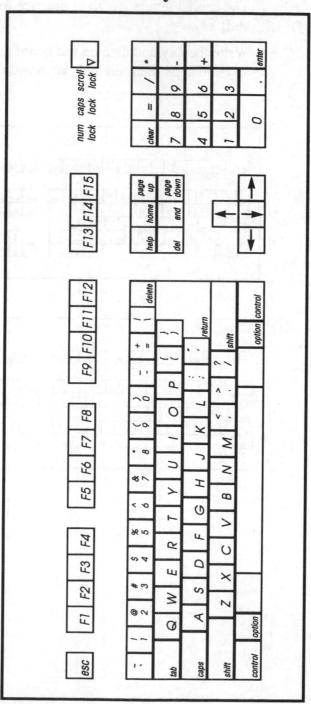

IBM and PC Compatible Keyboard

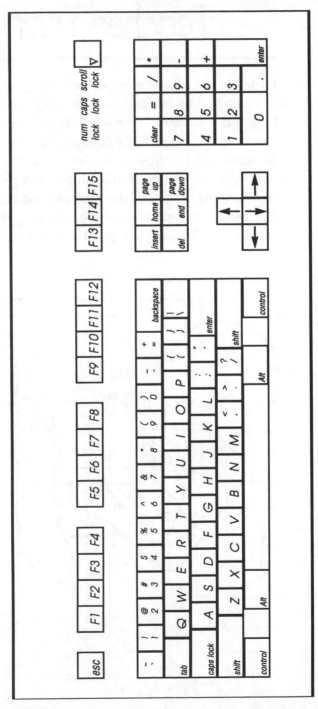

Using Kid Pix for Teacher Training

If you are a teacher trainer in technology or in the process of integrating technology into the curriculum, you will find this book invaluable. Use the A Walk Through *Kid Pix* as your introduction to *Kid Pix* and then have your trainees use several of the projects to show how *Kid Pix* can be used in the various academic areas. After your trainees have finished several of the projects, use this as a jumping-off place for a discussion of the vote of technology in the curriculum. Get ready! Get set! Go for an adventure!

Managing Your Classroom for Kid Pix

The One-Computer Classroom

The teacher in Room 1 says, "Get real! I only have one computer in my classroom. How am I supposed to use a program like *Kid Pix* with my 25 students?"

Let's explore some one-computer classroom configurations to help answer that question. First, determine how the computer should be used. Some questions to ask yourself:

1. Do I want my students to use the computer for projects?

2. Do I want to use the computer as a presentation tool?

3. How often will the computer be used by my students?

4. Do I want to use the computer for cooperative learning?

5. How can I set up the computer with my current electrical outlets?

6. What other equipment does the school possess that I can use with the computer?

   - Is there an overhead projector?

   - Is there a converter to use to connect to a TV?

   - Is there a TV set I can use in my classroom?

   - Is there an LCD panel I can use?

   - Are there any speakers that I can use?

   - Is there a printer for my classroom?

"I have asked everyone and found out there is no equipment other than my classroom computer for me to use."

Teacher Use in the One-Computer Classroom

If your computer has a monitor that can be separated from the central processing unit (CPU), place it higher than the table. You can even place it on chairs on top of a table. Raising the monitor will make it more accessible to your class. Just rearrange the seating a little to accommodate your class's viewing of the monitor.

You can use your computer as the center of a small-group lesson. Why not bring one of your math groups up to the computer area and have them sit on the floor or in chairs around the monitor? You know the rest of the class will lock their eyes onto the monitor, and your lesson will get double the exposure!

You may also want to invest in an inexpensive pair of speakers which can be found for around $20. Make sure the speakers are self-powered.

Student Use in the One-Computer Classroom

The computer can be used as part of a learning center environment by developing a good student-computer-use schedule. The key to success is planning and scheduling.

First, demonstrate to your class the project that you want them to create. Then place the computer on a table with supporting materials.

If you want your students to do a math project, have some illustrated math books available at the center, along with concrete materials that students can manipulate. If the center is located near a bulletin board, the board can be used to illustrate their final projects, or it can contain information useful in creating their projects.

Two students working at the computer or technology center can work in a very cooperative manner. While one student is planning, the other one can be inputting the material.

Use the printouts of the *Kid Pix* Rubber Stamps (pages 280–287) by mounting them on file folders and laminating them. Then, place them at the center for students to use as clip art reference. The printouts of the icons should be mounted and laminated for easy reference, as well. These laminated file folders will prove to be invaluable timesaving devices.

If you don't have a printer in your room, your students can save their materials to disks. Later, either you or your students can take their disks to a computer attached to a printer to print out their materials.

Note: The computer that is attached to the printer must have *Kid Pix* on the hard drive in order to print their projects. Remember, your printer need not be fancy to print out *Kid Pix* projects.

"Yes! My school does have a converter and an extra TV for me to use."

You are in luck.

You have two modes in which to use *Kid Pix*. You have a great setup to use *Kid Pix* in your classroom as a presentation tool to introduce skills and concepts, as well as to use the computer for individual students and small groups. The TV now becomes your electronic chalkboard. For example, you can easily illustrate a geometry lesson, teaching directly in front of your class. You know students will look at the TV screen. You won't even need to say, "Look up here now." They will just do it.

An example of a primary geometry lesson easily done with *Kid Pix* might be showing the difference between rectangles and squares.

Open the *Kid Pix* application and select the Rectangle tool. Draw some rectangles on the screen and ask the obvious question, "What sizes are the lines that make a rectangle?"

How easy it is for the students to see two lines the same size and then two other lines the same size, all four not being equal. Hold down the shift key and draw some squares and have them see the difference. You can use the projects in this book and show them in front of your class to teach color names and to further math concepts.

By making a slide show, you can create many presentations quickly to illustrate the concepts that you are teaching. In first grade, a slide show showing math combinations keeps your students' attention while you present math facts. (See pages 75–79 on how to make a slide show.)

Imagine a young student presenting a project to the entire classroom on a large TV. It is quite a self-esteem builder.

The Multicomputer Classroom

Some classrooms are fortunate enough to have four computers and a printer. With solid scheduling and planning, these computers can be used for presentations by you and your students, or in the case of *Kid Pix*, they can be used for various curricular projects. The printer should always be humming with publications.

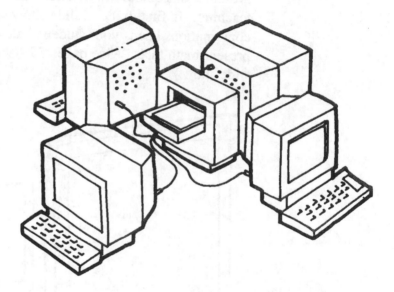

Scheduling time for students to work on the computer will always be an issue. There are many methods suggested for the one-computer classroom that will also work in the multicomputer classroom. However, differences do exist.

Scheduling your day in long, thematic blocks is probably the best way to utilize the computers in a minilab setting. It allows you to have students working on technology all day so the computers never sit idle. However, you still need to arrange your students and activities carefully to best use your time.

The projects in this book work well in the multicomputer classroom. The main issue is scheduling the time for your students to do their work. When creating your own technology projects, try to create projects that lend themselves to cooperative group activities. For example, create a project (or modify a lesson in this book) so that it has specific jobs. Each day, your students are assigned specific jobs they will perform during that day. Have your students use the Job Performance Record on page 294 to keep track of their contributions to their groups.

Using *Kid Pix* in the Computer Lab

Again, as in the classroom, it is planning and scheduling that makes the technology experience pleasant and productive for both students and teacher in the lab. The lab has an advantage over the classroom in the sense that all students can be working productively at the same time. More is produced over a shorter period of time.

It is essential in a lab situation that all students have their own disks for saving projects. Store these disks in a box that is carried to the lab from your classroom. As your students enter the lab, they collect their disks, sit at their computers, and are then ready to go. Review the instructions for saving work on the computer model in your school's lab.

Before turning your students loose on their own, be sure that you demonstrate the *Kid Pix* tools either on a large monitor or on a TV. If your school uses an LCD panel for large-screen demonstrations, you certainly can use it to preview *Kid Pix* for your students.

If students do their initial planning in the classroom and use their time in the computer lab for inputting their projects, then full use is made of their lab time. Use the printouts of the icons and rubber stamps on pages 280–292 in the classroom for your student projects. Use the *Kid Pix* Storyboard blackline master on page 296 liberally for the planning time in the classroom. These storyboards are great for small-group activities where all student team members can contribute to a project.

The projects in this book are easily adapted to the lab situation. Duplicate enough copies of a particular project so that all students have copies at their computers. Students then simply follow the directions, and the end products will show the results of their efforts in a very positive manner. As students get more proficient at manipulating the *Kid Pix* tools, you can make their projects more individualized.

Whatever your computer configuration, *Kid Pix* will be a delightful and productive program for your students to use.

Using Assessment in Kid Pix

Common understanding of authentic assessment is based upon assessing a student in a way that meets his/her learning style. Using technology for authentic assessment is a natural with *Kid Pix*. If we are to use Howard Gardner's theory of multiple intelligences from his book *Multiple Intelligences: The Theory into Practice** as a way to consider different learning abilities, then using *Kid Pix* as a basic tool follows easily. Gardner has currently identified seven intelligences. They are as follows:

1. **Linguistic**—engaged by working with words in games and through writing

2. **Logical-mathematical**—engaged by numbers, computers, and reasoning games

3. **Spatial**—engaged by artistic activities, reading maps and charts, solving jigsaw puzzles, and seeing patterns

4. **Musical**—engaged by listening to music and playing instruments; being aware of nonverbal sounds and patterns in speech and music

5. **Bodily-kinesthetic**—engaged by movement and sports activities; using body language for communication

6. **Interpersonal**—interested in working and learning in collaboration with other people

7. **Intrapersonal**—interested in working and learning alone

While reviewing the seven levels of multiple intelligences, you will be amazed by how many of these intelligences are encompassed in *Kid Pix*. The impact of using *Kid Pix* is most felt by the student who doesn't shine on the paper-and-pencil tests. Students can express their intelligence through creation and presentation, whereas normally the assessments are very confining. You might want to have your students use the self-assessment tool (page 295) as an attachment to their publications so that you can get a feeling for their own personal assessments.

*From *Multiple Intelligences: The Theory into Practice*, Howard Gardner. New York: Basic Books, 1993.

A Walk Through Kid Pix

This walk through *Kid Pix* merely shows you the basic capabilities of the program. As you try the various features, let yourself go and let the creativity flow.

There are some differences between *Kid Pix* and *Kid Pix Studio*. *Kid Pix* is a disk-based program, while *Kid Pix Studio* is only found on CD-ROM. You might have a copy of *Kid Pix*, *Kid Pix 2*, or *The New Kid Pix*. Directions which apply only to *Kid Pix* are noted as KP. When the directions are specifically for *Kid Pix Studio*, you will see KPS. This appears in the walk-through and in the student activity cards. *Kid Pix Studio* is addressed in detail on pages 92–129.

Now let's enter the fun world of *Kid Pix*. Follow along as we walk through the many features of *Kid Pix*.

To open the *Kid Pix* application, double-click on the *Kid Pix* icon.

You now have two menu bars, one to the left of the screen and one along the bottom of the screen. The menu on the left shows the available tools. The menu along the bottom shows tool options. There is also a large white area which is the *Kid Pix* drawing screen.

Select the Wacky Pencil by clicking on that tool. Move your mouse to the drawing screen.

The cursor, which is normally an arrow, has changed to a pencil. Notice that the Wacky Pencil icon in the TOOLS menu has been darkened. This means that it has been selected to be used. When you click on any icon, it will darken to show it is being used.

Using the Wacky Pencil:

Now that the Wacky Pencil tool has been selected, you need to select a color. Choose one of the colors from the Color Palette at the bottom of the left-hand menu bar.

Move the cursor onto the drawing screen, hold down the mouse button, and draw some squiggles on the screen. Then, select another color from the menu bar; but before you draw another picture, select the large line thickness from the menu along the bottom of the screen. Now you can draw another line.

Next, select the question mark from the menu along the bottom of the screen and draw something. Wow! Look at those colors! Finally, select one of the patterns from the menu along the bottom of the screen and draw. (See page 37 for samples of squiggles.)

If you don't like or no longer want the last item that you drew, just click The Undo Guy and your last step will disappear. You can also go to the EDIT menu and select Undo.

Now that the screen is full, you will need to erase it to get ready to experiment with some other tools.

Using the Eraser Tool:

Select the Eraser tool from the left-hand menu bar. Notice the bottom menu bar has changed to show different types of erasers. The first four erasers to the left are used for erasing small areas. The remaining erasers are used to erase an entire screen. Let's try the favorite of students everywhere. Select the firecracker and click on the drawing screen. It erases the entire screen.

Using the Line Tool:

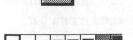

Select the Line tool. Then, select a color. Draw a line on the screen. Select another color and another line thickness. Now hold down the shift key and draw a line. Notice the line is straight. Select another color, line size, and pattern. Now try a few lines. (See page 38 for samples of lines.)

Clear the screen. Select the Eraser tool and choose one of the whole-screen erasers from the bottom menu. Click on the screen, and magically the screen is clear. You can also get a clear screen by going to the FILE menu and selecting New.

Using the Rectangle Tool:

Select the Rectangle tool from the left-hand menu. Then, select the question mark at the bottom of the screen. Hold your mouse button down and drag it diagonally to create a rectangle. Hold the shift key down while you draw the rectangle, and you will have a square. Select one of the patterns from the bottom menu bar and then choose a color. (See page 39 for samples of rectangles.)

Draw rectangles and squares. Remember, if you don't like the last thing you put on the screen, click The Undo Guy from the left-hand menu bar and it goes away. The Undo Guy takes away whatever was entered last.

Using the Oval Tool:

Select the Oval tool from the left-hand menu bar. Draw some differently colored circles. **Macintosh Users:** Hold down the option key while drawing in order to make a thicker border. Hold down the shift key to draw a perfect circle. **Windows Users:** Hold down the shift key to draw a perfect circle. Be sure to try different patterns from the Tool Options menu bar.

Select the Oval tool from the left-hand menu. Then select the Empty Box icon from the menu along the bottom of the screen. Draw a circle. (See page 40 for samples of circles.)

You are now going to fill your circle with color. Select the Paint Can tool from the left-hand menu. Then select a color. Move the Paint Can to the center of the circle and click the mouse button. Make some more circles and fill them, using different colors and patterns.

For an interesting drawing, select the Eraser tool, and then select one of the four erasers on the left. Move the mouse to the largest picture you have drawn. Then, hold down the mouse button inside the circle and draw your initials. Afterwards, clear your screen. (See page 41 for samples of initials.)

Using the Wacky Brush:

Select the Wacky Brush tool from the left-hand menu. Notice the tool options menu along the bottom of the screen changes. Let's try some of the options.

One at a time select each of the options to see what they do. You can change colors each time. Select the magnifying glass option. Move it over something you have already drawn, release the mouse, and the portion under the magnifying glass is enlarged.

Another way to clear the drawing area is to go to FILE menu and select New. Make sure you click on No in the dialogue box. (See page 42 for samples of magnifying glasses.)

Exploring the Wacky Brush Options:

Select the Wacky Brush tool from the menu. Then, click on the arrow to the far right of the menu bar along the bottom. The number will now show two. Let's explore the various tool options for the Wacky Brush. Select the tree option. Choose a color and then make some trees by holding down the mouse on the drawing screen. If you hold down the option key at the same time you are drawing trees, they will be really large. Clear the screen. (See page 43 for samples of trees.)

Select the Wacky Brush tool again, choose level two. Select the connect-the-dots option. Hold the mouse button as you go across the screen. You can make any shape dot-to-dot and choose any color. To better control the placement of the dots, release the mouse between each number. Clear the screen. (See page 44 for samples of dot-to-dots.)

More Exploring with the Wacky Brush Option:

With the Wacky Brush tool already selected, click on the arrow to the far right of the bottom menu bar until level two comes up. Select the Alphabet Line option.

Then, move the mouse around the drawing screen to make a dot-to-dot alphabet. (See page 45 for samples of alpha dot-to-dots.) Go to the GOODIES menu in KP and select Alphabet Text. Go to the TOOLBOX menu in KPS. The screen shows a dialogue box. The part that is highlighted can be changed.

Type in any words that you want your students to use as an outline for their drawing. Some suggestions: are color words, spelling words, animal words, etc. Click OK when finished. Select the Wacky Brush tool, level two, and the Alphabet tool. Hold down the mouse button and draw an object on the screen. This is a great way to reinforce spelling words. You can print it out for an activity sheet. Clear your screen; we have lots more to explore. (See page 46 for a sample of an alphabet picture.)

Using the Text Tool:

Select the Text tool from the left-hand menu. Along the bottom of the screen the alphabet appears. Scroll through the alphabet by clicking on the numbered arrow at the far right. You will also see numbers and punctuation marks. To use Spanish letters and sounds, go to the GOODIES menu in KP or the TOOLBOX menu in KPS and select Switch to Spanish. Notice the menu bar also changes to Spanish. Scroll through the alphabet by using the numbered arrow at the far right.

The appropriate punctuation marks will appear for Spanish.

Choose a letter and put it on the drawing screen. Notice that when you choose your letter, the letter and number names are said. You can write words in this manner. (See page 47 for samples of Spanish letters.)

Writing with the Text Tool:

There are other methods you can use to write on the screen. One way to write on the drawing screen is to use the option key and the Text tool together. Hold down the option key and select the Text tool at the same time. Notice that when you press the option key and click on the Text tool from the left-hand menu, you get a choice of letters along the bottom of the screen. Select one of the type styles, move to the drawing screen, and type in what you want. You must click on the screen before beginning to type, or you will wonder where the writing went.

You can also go to the GOODIES menu and select Type Text and then follow the same steps as above.

Select another color and type style from the menus to make a change, but you can only do this if you haven't clicked somewhere else on the screen.

Using the Rubber Stamp Options:

Select the Rubber Stamps tool from the left-hand menu. Notice that the Tool Option menu along the bottom of the screen changes yet again. At the far right side of the tool option menu are two arrows, one going up and one going down. Click these arrows to change to another group of rubber stamps. There are eight different levels.

Another selection of stamps can be obtained from the menu bar at the top of the screen. Go to the SWITCHEROO menu in KP and select Swap Stamps. Release the mouse button, and you will see on the screen many sets of stamps that are labeled. To get even more stamps, click on the down arrow at the far right of the screen and hold down your mouse button. In KPS, go to the GOODIES menu and select Pick a Stamp Set.

Choose a stamp group by double-clicking on a stamp. You now have more levels of stamps from which to choose. Click on one stamp. Click on the drawing screen. This is the smallest size of rubber stamp.

Changing Stamp Size:

Macintosh Users: To make the stamp one size larger, hold down the option key while clicking on the screen. Hold down the shift key while clicking on the screen for the next larger size. Hold down the option and the shift keys together to get the largest size possible. Choose a few more stamps and try them in different sizes.

Windows Users: Hold down the control or the control and shift keys together to change sizes of stamps. (See page 48 for samples of stamp sizes.)

Changing and Creating Stamps:

You can change existing rubber stamps or even create your own stamps in *Kid Pix*. Select the Rubber Stamp tool. Choose a stamp that you want to edit by clicking on that stamp.

In KP go to the GOODIES menu and select Edit Stamp. In KPS go to the TOOLBOX menu and select Edit Stamp. Your stamp is now very large on the screen.

Select a color and click on the stamp where you want the color to appear. Change direction by clicking on the right and left arrows to flip the stamp. Click OK, and your stamp will appear on the drawing screen. Go back to the GOODIES menu, select Edit Stamp, and then choose Restore Original. The original stamp is back.

When you go to quit the program, it will ask you if it should restore the stamps to the originals. (See page 49 for samples of editing stamps.)

Using the Electric Mixer:

To see the amusing effects of the electric mixer, make sure you have something drawn on the screen and then select Electric Mixer tool. Select one of the effects from the menu along the bottom of the screen and then click on the screen. Explore the various capabilities. (See page 50 for samples of electric mixers.)

Using the Moving Van:

Clear your screen. Use the tools you have explored and create a picture on the screen. Now let's move parts of the picture around. Select the Moving Van tool. Click on a shape in the tool option menu. Move the shape to the picture. Hold down the mouse button and move the shape to another part of the screen. Try different shapes. To customize the size to be moved, click on the magnet at the far right. Click on the screen and drag to the size you want to move. Hold the mouse down in the center of the shape and move it. (See page 51 for samples of moving vans.)

Using the Menu Bar:

KP Menu

File   Edit   Goodies   Switcheroo

KPS Menu

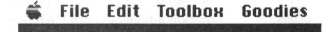

File   Edit   Toolbox   Goodies

Now you will look at the activities you can do using the menu bar located at the top of the screen.

Move your mouse arrow to the FILE menu and hold down the mouse button.

Selecting Print from the FILE menu brings up a dialogue box on the screen. In it you need to choose point size and the number of copies you want. If you are connected to an Imagewriter, the box will give an option to click for color or black and white. Be sure to click Imagewriter color or your students will be disappointed with their printouts.

As you look through your GOODIES menu, you will notice that there is a Record Sound option available. If you have a microphone or one is built into the hardware system, after your picture is complete, go to the GOODIES menu and select Record Sound. Click on Record, and you will have 32 seconds, which is a really long time, to tell about your picture.

In KP go to the SWITCHEROO menu and select Swap Hidden Pictures. In KPS go to the GOODIES menu and select Swap Hidden Pictures. Then select the Eraser tool from the left-hand menu, select the question mark, and erase the screen to reveal a fabulous picture. Hold the option key down at the same time, and a larger area of the screen is erased. (See page 52 for samples of hidden pictures.)

Select ColorMe from the SWITCHEROO menu to select from a series of black and white pictures that can be colored, printed, saved, and even used in a Slide Show. Put the very tip of the paint coming out of the Paint Can tool on a line and click. All the lines in the picture will change to that color. (See page 53 for samples of ColorMe.)

The DrawMe option in the SWITCHEROO menu presents ideas for starting picture stories.

The Wacky TV option in the SWITCHEROO menu lets you put movie segments into your stories. There will be a separate project showing you how to do this.

The last option in the SWITCHEROO menu is the Switch to Slide Show. We will do a separate project for you to create a slide show.

Samples of Squiggles

Samples of Lines

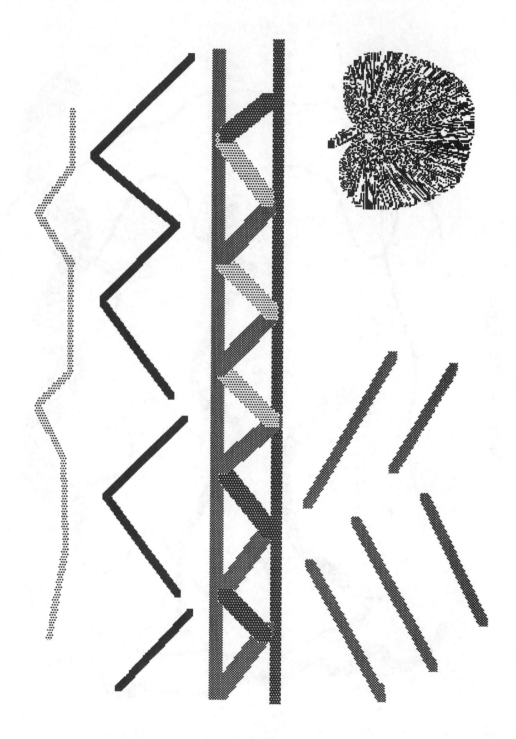

Samples of Rectangles

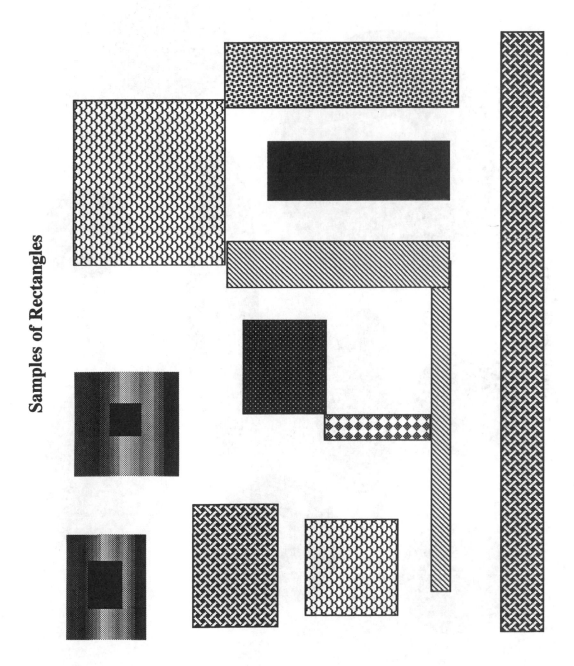

Samples of Circles

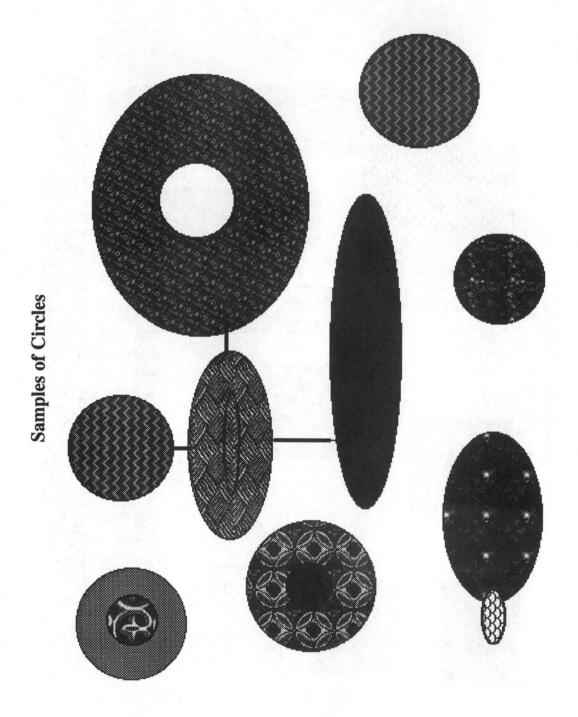

40

Samples of Initials

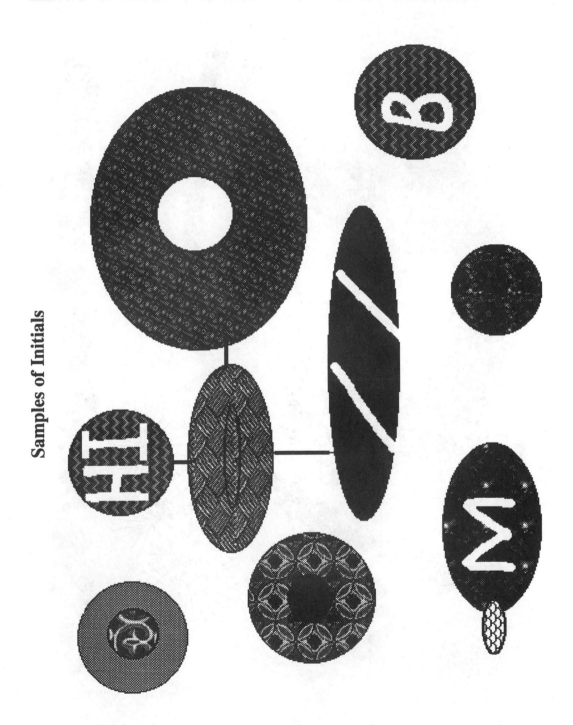

Samples of Magnifying Glasses

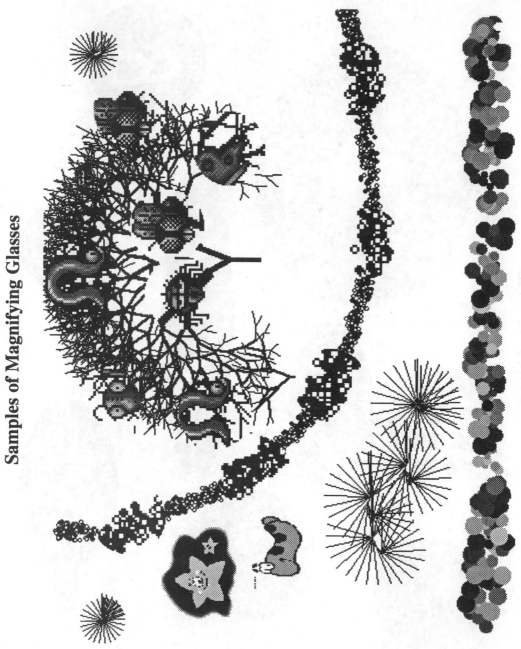

Samples of Trees

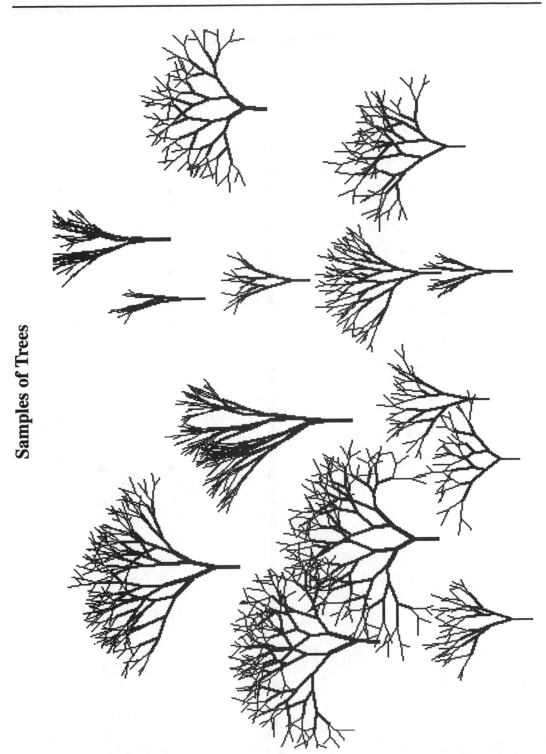

Samples of Dot-to-Dots

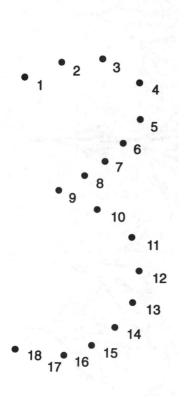

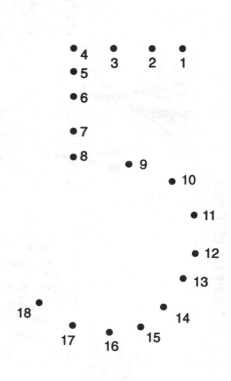

Samples of Alpha Dot-to-Dots

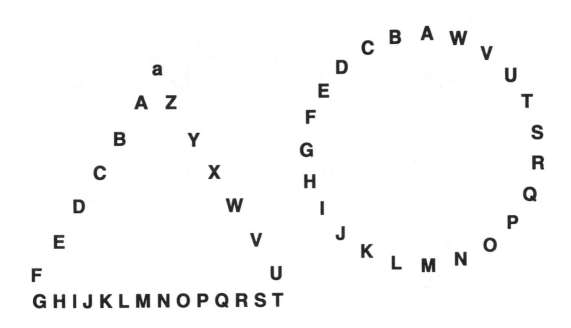

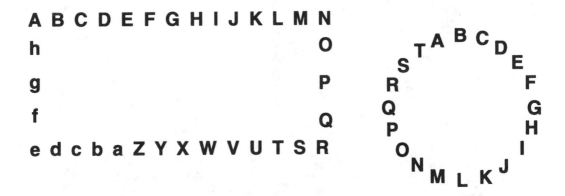

Samples of Alphabet Picture

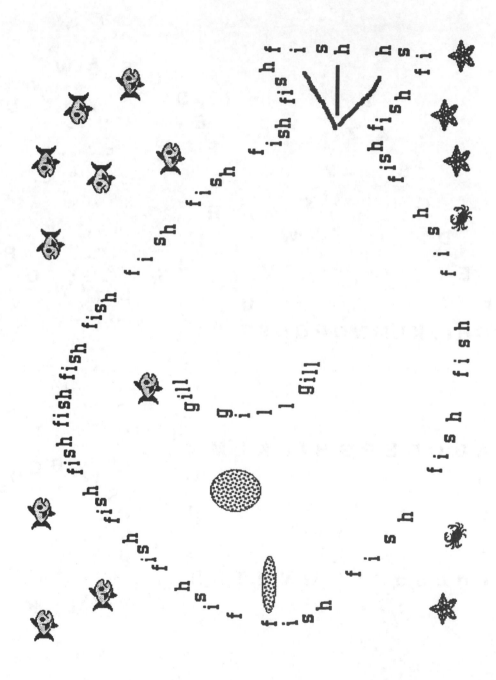

Samples of Spanish Letters

NIÑO

¿COMO ESTA?

ELLA

¡HOLA!

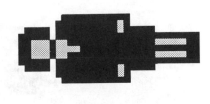

Samples of Stamp Sizes

Yum, yum!

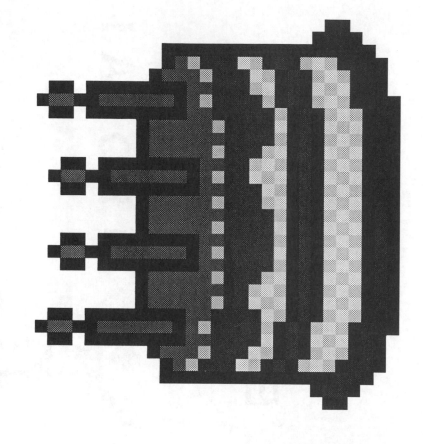

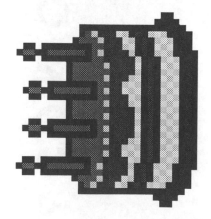

Samples of Editing Stamps

Samples of Electric Mixers

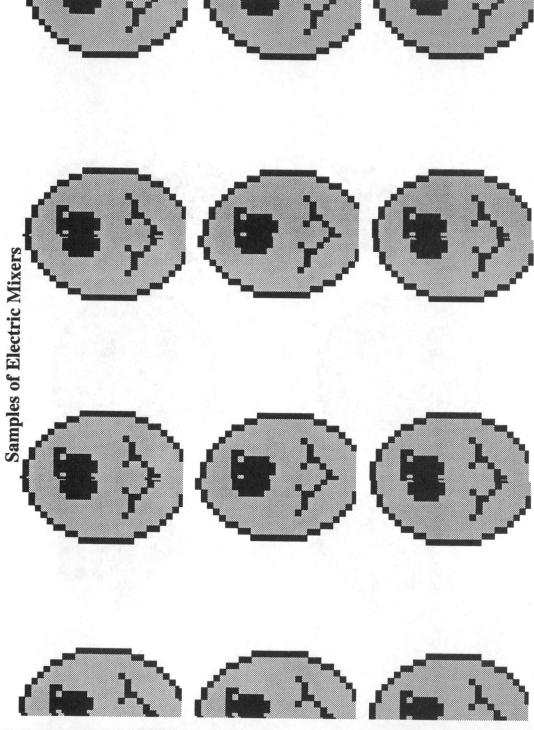

50

Samples of Moving Vans

Samples of Hidden Pictures

52

Samples of ColorMe

Kid Pix Teacher Project—My Vacation Hideaway

Drawing a Picture:

1. Select the Wacky Pencil tool from the left-hand menu.

2. Select a green color from the palette.

3. Go to the far left of the screen with your Wacky Pencil tool, hold down the mouse button, and draw a mountain outline all the way across to the other side of the screen. Be sure both sides of the mountain touch the edges of the screen.

4. Select the Paint Can tool from the left-hand menu. Move the paint can inside the mountain and click. The mountain fills with whatever color you have chosen.

5. Select the Rubber Stamps tool from the left-hand menu. Click the number arrow until you get to level two. Select a tree stamp and place some trees on the mountain.

Macintosh Users: Remember that using the option, shift, or option/shift keys together changes the sizes of the stamps. **Windows Users:** Hold down the control or the control/shift keys together to change the sizes of stamps. (See page 56 for sample picture of trees on mountain.)

6. Click to level four of the Original Stamp Set and choose the house to put in your picture. In KP go to the SWITCHEROO menu and select the City grouping to find some more trees to add to your picture. In KPS go to the GOODIES menu and select Pick a Stamp Set.

7. You may want to choose the Wacky Pencil tool, the color blue, and a thick line and draw in a stream. When you want to use rubber stamps, be sure you click on the Rubber Stamps tool first. (See page 57 for a sample picture of a mountain stream.)

8. Use the Rubber Stamps tool and options to complete your illustration.

Sample Picture of Trees on Mountain

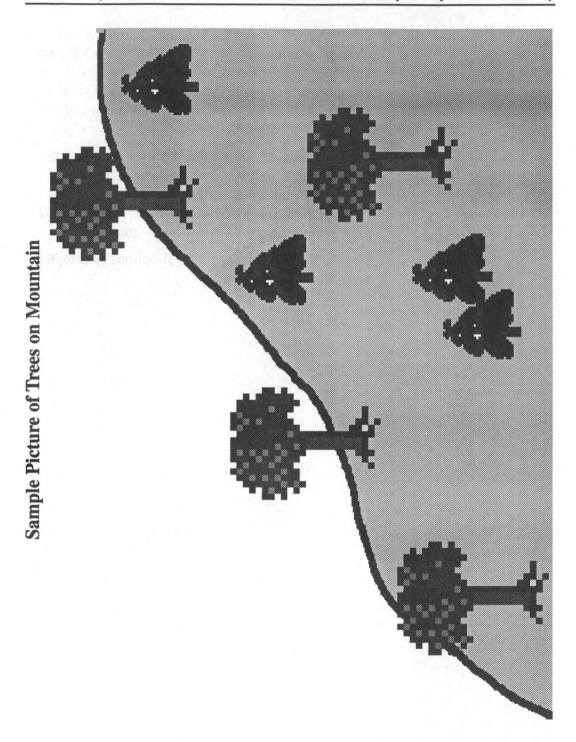

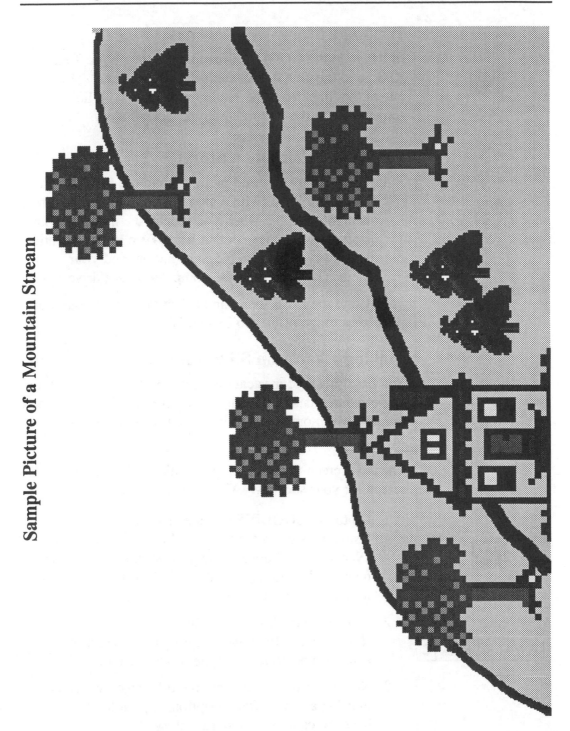

Sample Picture of a Mountain Stream

Writing a Story:

In KP go to the GOODIES menu and select Type Text. In KPS go to the GOODIES and select Typewriter. Choose one of the fonts from the Tool Options menu. Click somewhere on the picture and type in your story.

Saving and Printing a Story:

1. To save the story and picture, go to the FILE menu and select Save. The dialogue box shows an area that is highlighted so when you type in the name of your story, it will appear in that box. Type in My Vacation Hideaway. Click on the Save button, and your picture is saved onto the computer's hard drive.

2. Go to the FILE menu and select Print, and your story goes to the printer to be published.

Making a Vacation Slide Show:

You have saved your vacation story, and that is going to be one of your slides in the slide show presentation. You need to make two more slides to include in your Vacation Slide Show.

The next screen you are going to make will be the title screen for your show, My Vacation Hideaway.

1. Go to the GOODIES menu and select Type Text. Using KPS go to the GOODIES menu and select Typewriter. Choose the largest point size from the menu. Click in the middle left of the screen and type in My Vacation Hideaway.

2. To give yourself credit as the creator of this slide show, click in the lower right-hand corner, select another type style, and type in your name.

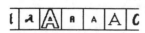

3. Now it is time to decorate the title page. Be creative in using all the different options available. If you have the capability, record a story about your vacation.

4. Save the title page. Go to the FILE menu and select Save. Type in the name Title. You now have the title screen to the slide show. Clear the screen by using the Eraser tool from the left-hand menu or go to the FILE menu and select New.

5. For the third screen, show how you get to the hideaway. For this presentation, let's go there by train.

6. Go to the SWITCHEROO menu, select Swap Stamps, and choose the city. Pick some of the railroad cars and place them on your screen.

7. To make straight tracks, choose the Line tool from the left-hand menu and hold down the shift key as you draw.

8. Write some information about the train trip.

9. Save this page as Train to Vacation.

Now it is time to put these pictures together into a slide show.

Putting Your Slide Show Together:

You now have three screens saved:

   -Title page

   -My Vacation Hideaway screen

   -Train to Vacation screen

You will now put them all together.

1. Go to the SWITCHEROO menu and select Switch to Slideshow. On the screen is a series of moving vans. Each one represents one screen in the slide show. The screen shows 12 vans, but if you use the down arrow at the far right-hand corner, you can find 99 vans, which means that you can have up to 99 slides in a slide show. It is best to put all of the pictures that you want together into one folder so that they will be easy to access.

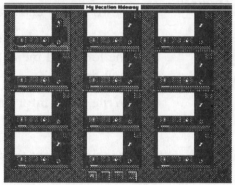

2. Click on the first icon on the left under the truck. This is the Pick a Picture! button used to place the picture. Your first slide will be the title page. On your screen should be a listing of things you have saved. Find title page and double-click. Your title will now be the picture on the van.

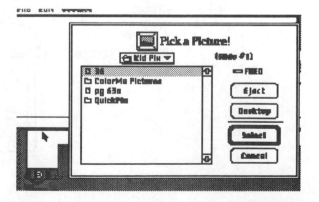

3. The second icon, Pick a Sound!, is for the sound. Click on the second icon. From this screen you can pick prerecorded sounds, or you can select the microphone and record your story. This works only if you have a microphone with your computer. Select a sound and choose Preview to hear it. When you find a sound that you like, click on Select.

4. The third icon is for you to choose a transition screen. Click on one and then preview to see how it looks. Use Select to choose your transition. There is no transition after the last picture.

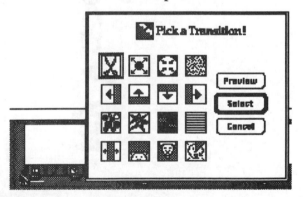

Repeat this process with the next two moving vans to produce your slide show.

If you want to change the order of your slides, click on a van, and while holding down your mouse button, move to another place.

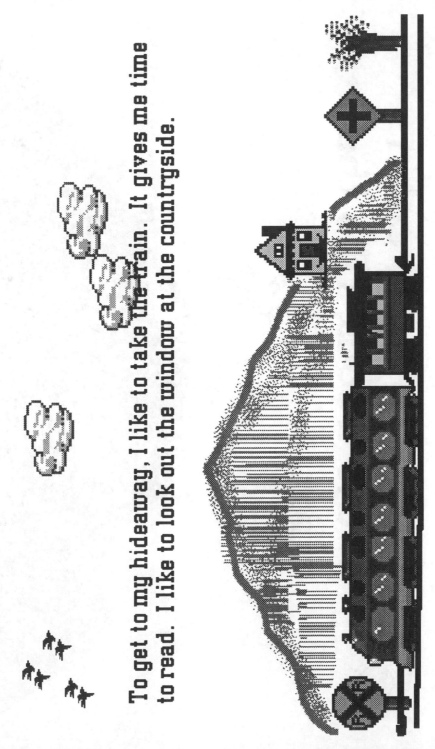

To get to my hideaway, I like to take the train. It gives me time to read. I like to look out the window at the countryside.

When summer vacation is here, I go to my cabin in the woods. I like the quiet.

Marian Adams

Importing a Photo from a Disk into Kid Pix

Importing a picture into *Kid Pix* is a very easy process. All you need is a disk on which your pictures have been developed. There are several companies that process pictures onto disks (e.g., Konica, Seattle Film Works, etc.). The envelopes for these companies are available at many photo processing centers. Simply send your film to the company of your choice and make sure you have marked the envelope(s) correctly to have them developed onto disks. You can also order prints at the same time. When the disk is returned, view your photos and save the ones you like onto your hard drive. Another way to save and organize your photos is to place them on a separately labeled disk.

1. Put a disk into the hard drive and move the saved pictures from the hard drive to the disk by clicking the title of the picture and holding down your mouse button while moving the picture to the disk.

2. Organize your photos by using a disk for each category, such as "A Field Trip to the Zoo" or photos of classroom presentations.

Now that your photos are organized, it is time to import them into *Kid Pix*.

1. Open *Kid Pix*.

2. Select Open from the FILE menu.

3. You now have to tell the computer where the picture is located.

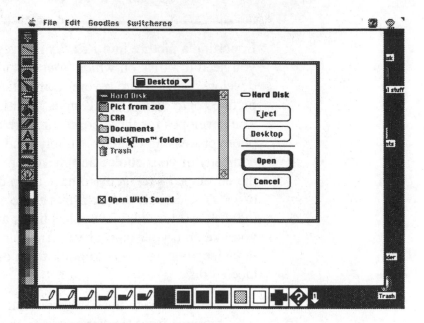

4. Double-click on the title of the picture you want.

5. Your choice is now on the screen.

6. Use the Rubber Stamp tool to add objects to the picture.

7. Select Type Text from the GOODIES menu to write anything you want on the picture.

8. Print the picture.

A Day at the Zoo

Importing a Picture from Kid Pix into The Writing Center

1. Open *The Writing Center* and choose which format you need to use.

2. A blank screen will appear. Select Choose a Picture from the PICTURE menu.

3. You need to tell the computer where your picture is located.

4. Find your picture and double-click to open it. If it is in a file, double-click to open the file. Click on the name of the picture you want to open.

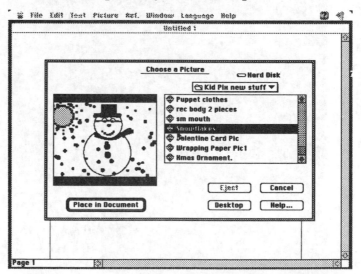

5. Click on the Place in Document button.

6. Your picture will appear on the screen in full size. To make it smaller, select Resize Picture from the PICTURE menu. Click on the circle in front of To Half Original Size. Then click Done.

7. Your picture will now appear in a smaller size on the screen. You can move it over to the middle or anywhere else by putting your mouse button in the middle of the picture and holding the button down while moving the picture.

8. To make a frame around your picture, select Border from the PICTURE menu. Click on Triple Line in the Border Lines selections and then click OK.

9. To begin your writing, just click your mouse at the top of the page and use the return key to move the cursor down. Write your text. Remember, you can use the TEXT menu to change fonts and styles.

Importing a Picture from Kid Pix into MS Works

You are going to learn how to bring a picture made in *Kid Pix* into a *Microsoft Works* document. The directions for this procedure will work with almost any word processing program.

To bring a picture into a word processor at the top of the page, follow these steps:

1. Open your word processor to a blank screen. You are now ready to bring in a picture.

2. Select Open from the FILE menu. Then tell the computer where the picture is that you want to bring in (e.g., hard drive, disk, desktop, etc.).

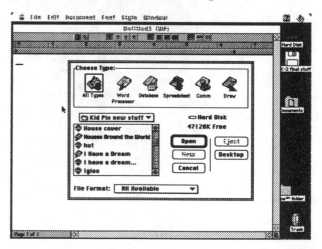

3. Double-click on the name of the picture you want to import.

4. The picture appears on the screen, and now you can edit the picture to make it smaller, or you can even crop it.

5. Click the mouse in the middle of your picture, and small black handles will appear.

6. To make the picture smaller, click on the handle in the upper left-hand corner and drag it diagonally. To move the picture up, click in the middle of the picture, hold down the mouse button, and move the picture wherever you want it.

7. Move it onto the page where you want it to appear.

8. Select Copy from the EDIT menu. The computer needs to know where to copy it.

9. Close your screen, and when asked if you want to save it, select No.

10. Click on the blank screen and select Paste from the EDIT menu. Your picture is now on the screen.

11. If you click on the picture, the handles will reappear, and you can edit the picture more.

12. To write under your picture, turn off the drawing tools by closing the drawing tools box. Your cursor should be in the upper left-hand corner. Use the return key to move the cursor down under the picture.

13. Write the text that you want. Remember that you can highlight the text and change the fonts and styles. (See page 72 for an example picture of the above procedure.)

Example of a Picture That Has Been Brought into *MS Works*

Here is a picture of my aquarium that I drew all by myself. The fishes are swimming around the castle, and the starfish are hanging around on the bottom.

Writing, Developing, and Producing a Slide Show in a Small Group

Creating a slide show is an inspiring way to introduce students to multimedia production. Working together, students learn the steps involved in the development of a multimedia project. They will learn to use a storyboard, set goals, work together as a team, and adhere to a schedule, as well as working in their special areas of talent.

Forming Groups

Groups are formed either by teacher choice or at random. The subject of the slide show is discussed in a whole class situation, and then the groups meet on their own.

Telling a Story

- Groups brainstorm on the contents of their stories.
- With one group member acting as a scribe, they then write their stories.
- Once the story has been written, it now needs to be charted on a storyboard so that the sequence of the story and the graphics needed are organized. You could have each student do an individual storyboard or provide a large-sized one on butcher paper that can be used as a group storyboard.

Assigning Tasks Within the Group

- When a storyboard is completed, the group assigns tasks for its production. There needs to be an artist or artists who will make the final decision on the graphics and eventually place them on the screen.

Assigning someone to do the typing of the text is also very important. Group members have to decide on the transitions and audio for their story. The group may have decided on using tapes or CDs as background music, and the appropriate music has to be obtained by the sound people. One group member needs to be assigned to compile all of the scenes into one slide show.

- Another method of production is for the group to divide into smaller units so that each screen has an assigned group of producers.
- The group then is assigned a time to use the computer or computers for inputting the graphics, text, sound, transitions, etc.

Putting It Altogether

- One student in the group compiles all of the screens into one slide show. The group views the slide show and comments on changes to be made. In *Kid Pix* it is very easy to move slides. Just place the mouse cursor in the middle of the moving van and while holding down the mouse button, move it to another place.

Viewing the Project

- The slide show can be saved as a Stand Alone and then shown on any computer that has the same hardware as the one on which it was created.
- The slide show can also be saved as a Movie if you are using *Kid Pix Studio* and then placed into a *Kid Pix* screen.
- Students present their slide shows to the class. It is great fun to have students show their projects at Back to School Night or Open House. Parents will be amazed at their children's productions.

Creating a Slide Show for the Primary Classroom

Producing a slide show to use with your students provides you with two different mediums of presentation: book and multimedia. If you print out each page as it is created, you can assemble your slide shows into a classroom book.

Middle grade students should be able to create this slide show, using the directions on the following pages.

Before you begin creating slides for your own slide show, set up a folder or subdirectory for all of your work. Each time you save a slide, it goes into your own folder or subdirectory. This way all your slides are together so that when you want to use them, they are all in the same place. **Macintosh Users:** Before opening *Kid Pix*, select New Folder from the FILE menu. New Folder will appear on the screen either darkened or highlighted. When you type in a title for your folder, it will appear on the screen. A suggested title might be your name and the subject of your slide show. **Windows Users:** Before opening *Kid Pix*, select Open from the FILE menu. Next, select the drive you want your new folder to be placed on and click File Options. Finally, click New Directory and type in a name for your new folder. A suggested title might be your name and the subject of your slide show.

The following slide show example will be teaching about the life cycle of the butterfly.

Making a Title Screen:

Open *Kid Pix* and select Type Text from the GOODIES menu. If you are using KPS, select the Typewriter Tool from the TOOLS menu. Choose a font from the bottom of the screen. Then click on the middle of the screen and type in the title, "How a Butterfly Develops," press return four times, and then type in your name as the author.

Decorate your title page with various aspects of the butterfly cycle. Select the Rubber Stamp tool. Looking at the bottom of the screen, choose the stamps that represent butterflies and place them on your title page screen. Select Swap Stamps from the SWITCHEROO menu. Remember you can vary the size of each stamp. **Macintosh Users:** Hold down the shift, option, and command keys to change the size of your stamps. **Windows Users:** Hold down the control and shift keys to change stamp sizes.

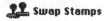
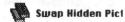

Saving Your Slide to a Folder:

Choose Save As from the FILE menu. You now have to tell the computer where your folder is located. If you have a Macintosh, click on Desktop and Open Document to find your folder. It might also be found on the hard drive or an external drive.

If you are using *Windows*, choose Open from the FILE menu and then select the drive you saved your folder onto. When you find your folder, and after you have opened it, title your slide "Slide #1 Butterfly Cycle." Click on Save. (See pages 81 and 82 for samples of a title slide.)

Clear the screen to make your second slide. You can use the Eraser tool or choose New from the FILE menu.

Second Slide:

Use the Wacky Pencil tool to draw a branch with a leaf and an egg. Use any of the drawing tools to complete your picture.

Select the Typewriter tool if you are using KPS, or if you are using KP, select the Alphabet Text option from the GOODIES menu and choose a small font. Type in the following:

A butterfly passes through four stages. This process is called metamorphosis. The four stages are egg, caterpillar, chrysalis, larva or pupa, and, finally, butterfly.

Remember, if you make a mistake, you can erase by clicking on the Eraser tool on the left side of the screen. Then select the smallest eraser from the bottom far left of the options menu.

When you are finished, select Save As from the FILE menu. Your folder should appear on the screen. Type in Slide #2 Four Stages and click Save. (See page 83 for a sample of slide #2.)

Clear the screen to make your third slide. You can use the Eraser tool or select New from the FILE menu.

Slide Three:

Choose the caterpillar from the Rubber Stamps. Place it on the screen in large format (size). You may have to draw a caterpillar if there is not one in your rubber stamps choices.

Choose the Alphabet Text tool from the GOODIES menu in KP or the Typewriter tool in KPS. Label the different parts of the caterpillar.

Select Save As from the FILE menu and title the screen Slide #3 Caterpillar. (See page 84 for a sample of slide #3.)

Clear the screen to make your fourth slide. You can use the Eraser tool or select New from the FILE menu.

Slide Four:

Use the Wacky Pencil tool to draw a branch and your chrysalis. Add the text to the bottom of the screen.

Select the Typewriter tool in KPS or the Alphabet Text tool from the GOODIES menu in KP and type in the text.

Select Save As from the FILE menu and title the screen Slide #4 Chrysalis. (See page 85 for a sample of slide #4.)

Slide Five:

Use the Wacky Pencil to draw a butterfly. Remember, if you make a mistake, you can use the Eraser tool or select the Undo Guy on the left side of the screen.

Select the Typewriter tool from KPS or the Alphabet Text tool from the GOODIES menu in KP. Now you can label the parts of the butterfly.

Select Save As from the FILE menu and title the screen Slide #5 Butterfly. (See page 86 for a sample of slide #5.)

Putting Your Slides Together into a Butterfly Slide Show

Select SlideShow from the SWITCHEROO menu in KP. Using KPS select SlideShow from the main menu. You will now see a series of moving vans. The first one is automatically highlighted.

Click on the first icon to the left. This will let you pick a picture to place in your slide show. Find your folder and open it. Double-click on title slide. (See page 87 for the Pick a Picture! screen.)

The picture that you picked will now appear in the van. Next, click the icon under the van which has a musical note on it. This is where you pick a sound to go with your picture. To hear the different sounds, select one and then click the Preview button. When you find one you like, click on Select. If you have a microphone attached to your computer or one is built in, you can record your own sound. (See page 88 for the Pick a Sound! screen.)

Click on the third button to the right to select a transition. Choose one you like and then click on Select. This will be the transition to the next slide. (See page 89 for the Pick a Transition! screen.)

Click on the picture icon in the second van and select Slide #2. Next, click on the sound icon and select a sound. Finally, click on the transition icon and select a transition.

Click on the picture icon in the third van and select Slide #3. Repeat the sound and transition procedures.

Click on the picture icon in the fourth van and select Slide #4. Repeat the sound and transition procedures.

Click on the picture icon in the fifth van and select Slide #5. Repeat the sound and transition procedures.

To play your slide show, click on the right arrow button at the bottom of the page. (See page 90 for a sample of a slide show.)

Creating a Science Slide Show for the Elementary Classroom

Saving Your Butterfly Slide Show

There are several ways in which to save your slide show, using the file menu. They are a stand alone, a slide show, or a movie.

1. Saving it as a slide show saves your work so that you can show it as a slide show or open it up and edit any of the slide show elements.

2. Saving it as a stand alone lets you save your work as a digital movie that can be copied to a computer's hard drive and played without KPS. Your slide show will run independently on any hardware that is the same as was used in the creation of your slide show. You may need to limit the number of slides or the amount of sound when you are saving to a floppy disk, as the sound takes up a lot of disk space.

3. Saving it as a QuickTime movie or an AVI (Audio-Video Interleave) allows you to save your work in a digital movie format which can be imported into another screen. (See page 91 for an example on importing and viewing a slide show.)

Sample of a Title Slide

The Story of a Butterfly

A butterfly passes through four stages. This process is called metamorphosis. The four stages are egg, caterpillar, chrysalis, larva, or pupa, and then butterfly.

Sample of a Title Slide

Text by Tom Smith
Design by Alexis Lee

How the Butterfly Developes

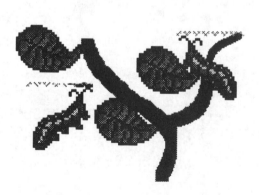

Sample of Slide #2

A butterfly passes through four stages. This process is called metamorphosis. The four stages are egg, caterpillar, (larva), chrysalis (pupa), butterfly.

Sample of Slide #3

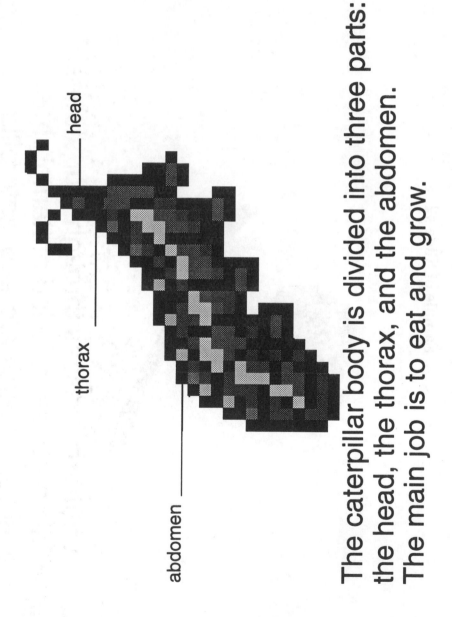

head

thorax

abdomen

The caterpillar body is divided into three parts: the head, the thorax, and the abdomen. The main job is to eat and grow.

Sample of Slide #4

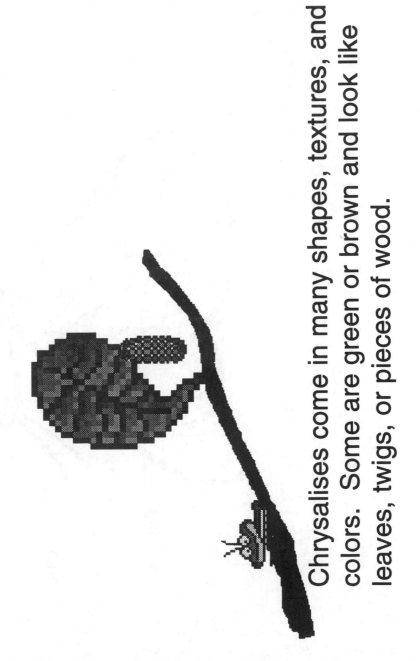

Chrysalises come in many shapes, textures, and colors. Some are green or brown and look like leaves, twigs, or pieces of wood.

Sample of Slide #5

The butterfly crawls out of the chrysalis. It usually has a short life of about two weeks, but some live six to eight months.

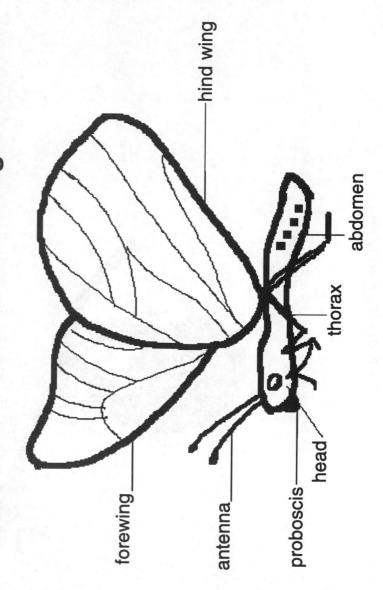

hind wing

abdomen

thorax

forewing

antenna

proboscis

head

Pick a Picture! Screen

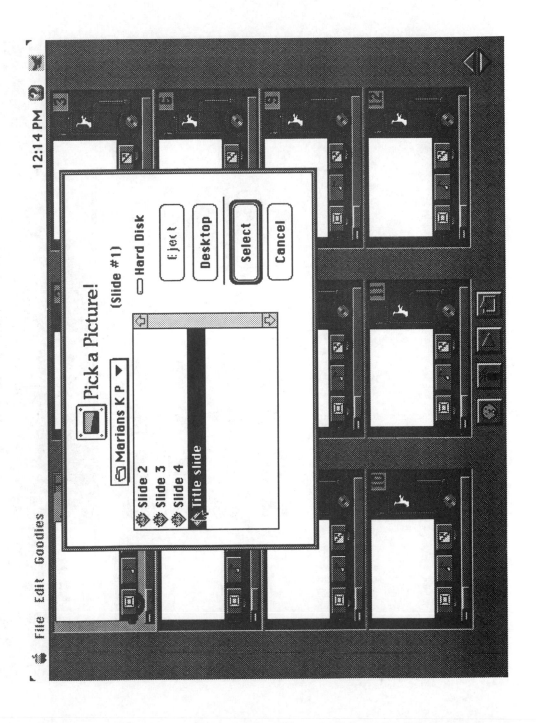

Pick a Sound! Screen

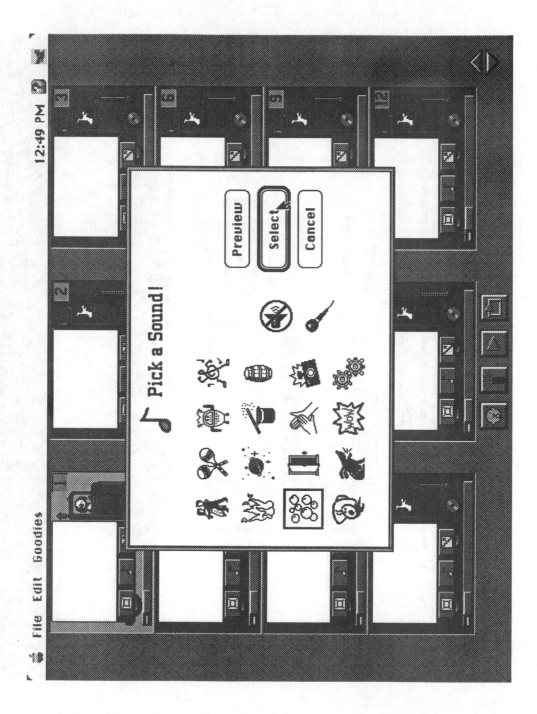

Pick a Transition! Screen

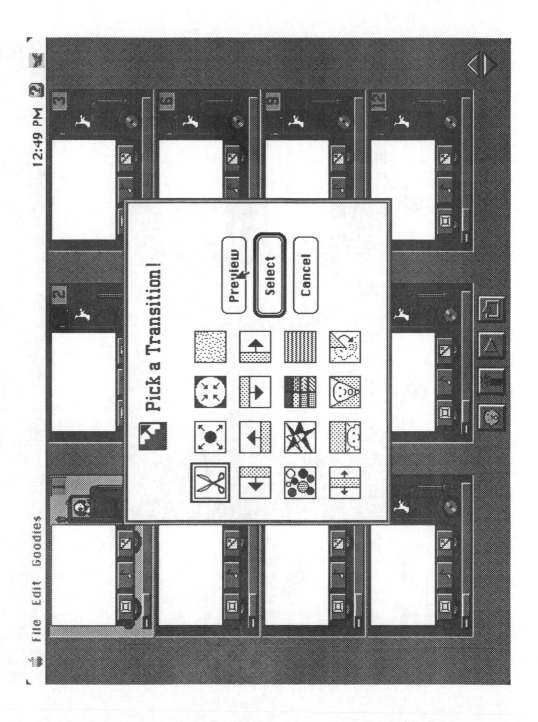

Sample of a Slide Show

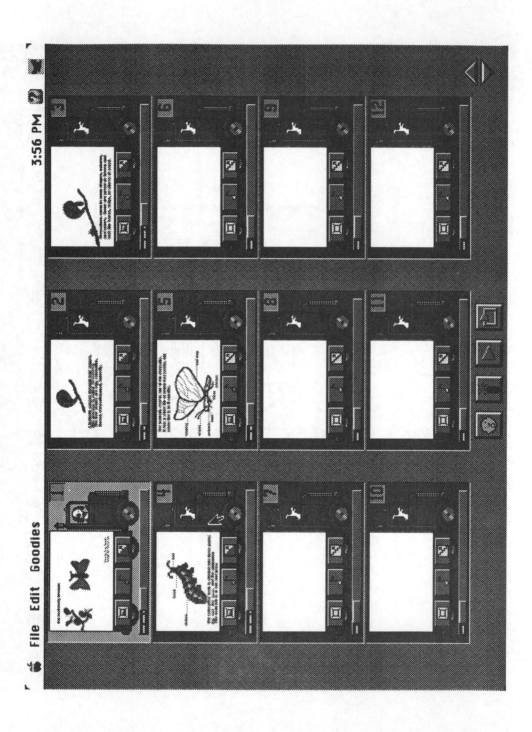

An Example of Importing and Viewing a Slide Show

Kid Pix Studio Features

Kid Pix Studio is a CD-ROM based computer program, available for the Macintosh and Windows platforms, that enlarges on the capabilities of the original disk-based *Kid Pix*. If you are using *Kid Pix Studio* with your students, you can use all the projects in this book. Just look for KPS for indications of slightly different options to use.

Kid Pix Studio contains the original *Kid Pix*, Wacky TV, and the capability to make a SlideShow. In addition it includes the following:

- Moopies
- Digital Puppets
- Stampimator

On the following page is a short preview of the six buttons on the *Kid Pix Studio* opening screen:

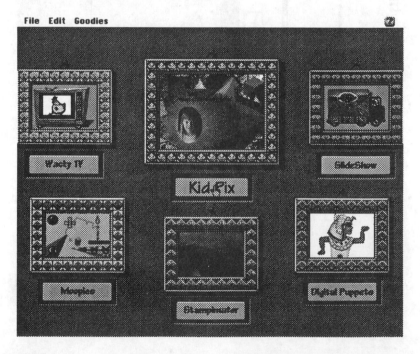

Kid Pix includes all the wonderful features and options of the disk version.

Moopies allows the creation of animations with "moving pictures."

Stampimator animates any stamp in *Kid Pix Studio* by dragging it over a path.

Digital Puppets Controls on-screen marionettes by the keys on the keyboard.

Slide Show links as many as 99 picture screens together in a continuous multimedia presentation.

Wacky TV makes 100 digital video clips available for use in *Kid Pix* pictures.

Kid Pix Studio Originals

Moopies Creations: Making Animated Stamps

Use the *Kid Pix* drawing tools to create a drawing. When you select Moopies, the menu is enhanced somewhat. Clicking on the Dancing Alphabet tool and placing the letter in the drawing makes moving letters.

In Moopies there is a choice among Animated Rubber Stamps. Choose from Toonies 1, 2, and the Teeny Toons stamp set to get animated stamps. You can also edit the stamps. (See page 95 for a picture of the Moopies screen.)

Stampinator Projects: Choosing Scenes, Actors, and Sound for Shows

Create your own background or choose one from the GOODIES menu (e.g., Pick a Background!). Once your background is ready, you can select up to four actors for your production. Choose from over 800 Rubber Stamps. (See page 96 for a picture of the Stampimator screen.)

Select the Rubber Stamps tool and then the first cast box. Click on the Rubber Stamps tool to select it. Click on a spot on the drawing screen, move across the screen, and the stamp will move along that path. Explore the Behavior buttons, Ping Pong button, Mirror Motion, and the Always Move button.

Digital Puppets: Creating Computer Marionettes

Choose a puppet from the Digital Puppet screen or go to the GOODIES menu and select Pick a Puppet. You can also select Pick a Sound! or Pick a Background! from the GOODIES menu. Digital Puppets can also be placed in a *Kid Pix* picture by selecting Import from the FILE menu. (See page 97 for a picture of the Digital Puppet screen.)

Screen Shot of the Moopies Screen

Screen Shot of the Stampimator Screen

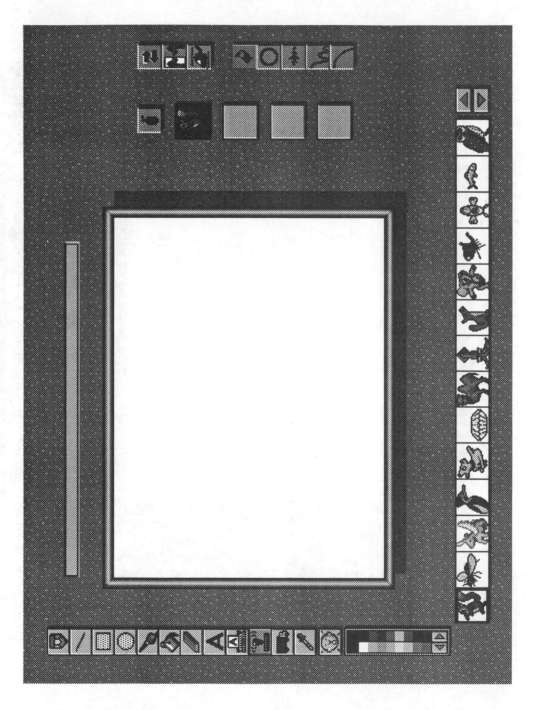

Screen Shot of the Digital Puppet Screen

A Walk Through Kid Pix Studio

There are several differences between *Kid Pix* and *Kid Pix Studio*, the main one being that *Kid Pix* is a disk-based program while *Kid Pix Studio* is CD-ROM based. The walk-through on pages 26–64, takes you through the disk-based *Kid Pix* (KP) program. This walk-through will show you the additional tools and options that are available in *Kid Pix Studio* (KPS). Use the walk-through for *Kid Pix* and keep this *Kid Pix Studio* walk-through handy to help you in your exploration.

Using the Wacky Pencil:

Click on the Wacky Pencil tool.

Next, select one of the colors shown in the Color Palette on the bottom left part of the screen. Notice how the color you have chosen appears at the top of the palette.

The line widths at the bottom of the screen, as well as the patterns, have also assumed the color you chose. Select one of the line widths and then, holding down the mouse button, make a drawing.

Clear the screen so you can try some more of the tools and options available. To do this, select New from the FILE menu and click No when asked if you want to save your previous drawing. You now have a clean drawing screen.

Click on the right arrow at the bottom of the color palette. You will see a new selection of colors. Keep clicking on the arrow to see all the possible choices of color. Select another color that you like, as well as a different pattern.

With your new pattern selected, draw something new on the drawing screen. **Note:** The white circle pattern acts as an eraser.

Select the Tint option and move over one of the lines that you have drawn. Watch how the color changes. Now try clicking on the question mark and then click on the screen and look at the colors. Clear your screen to try something new.

You are now going to try some really neat effects. Select a color from the Color Palette. Hold down the apple and command keys. Use the control and shift keys. Click the mouse on the screen and draw. This time hold down the apple, command, and shift keys for another effect. Click on the down arrow at the far right of the screen for more pattern choices. Now experiment with the apple, command, and the shift keys on the drawing screen. Hold down your mouse button while drawing continuously across the screen. Wow! The following section is another way to clear the drawing screen.

Using the Eraser Tool:

Select the Eraser tool. You will have a few more full screen erasers to choose from than in the original *Kid Pix*. The small erasers are slightly different.

Using the Line Tool:

To create some interesting changes in patterns, you can hold down the option key while drawing, you can hold down the apple and command keys, or you can hold down the apple, command, and shift keys together.

Using the Rectangle Tool:

Click on the down arrow at the far right of the screen to see the many levels of choices for patterns. Choose a pattern you like and hold down the mouse button while you drag the mouse across the screen to make a square. Fill the screen with rectangle and square shapes, using a different pattern each time. (See page 105 for samples of rectangles and squares.)

Clear the screen so that you can try some more of the *Kid Pix Studio* tools and options.

Using the Oval Tool:

Click on the Oval tool and create several circles and ovals on the screen. Use different fills with the Paint Can tool and fill each circle and oval you have created. (See page 106 for samples of circles and ovals.)

Using the Wacky Brush:

Explore the options of the Wacky Brush tool. Click on the arrows at the right of the menu bar to find the many different levels from which to choose. Hold down the option and shift keys, the apple and command keys, or the control keys as you explore. Hold down the control and shift keys as you draw.

Some highlights in the options menu are the following:

- **Three-Dimension Option** —This makes three-dimensional lines; try writing numbers and words with this tool. Hold down the apple and command keys as you write. (See page 107 for samples of three-dimensional pictures.)

- **Bug Option** —Hold down the apple and command keys and click bugs around the border of the screen. This will make a cool looking border. (See pages 108 and 109 for samples of bug frames.)

- **Hand Option** —Hold down the apple and command keys and move the mouse around the screen. (See page 110 for a sample hand frame.)

- **Number Option** —Write multiplication problems at random. Hold down the mouse button for four counts to get a multiplication problem without an answer. Hold down the mouse button for five counts to get a multiplication problem with an answer. (See page 111 for sample math problems.)

- **Build a House Option** —Create a picture of a house and its surroundings with the options on this level. (See page 112 for sample picture of a house.) To build the house from logs, click each log into place.

- **Humorous Option** —Enjoy finding the fun options on this level. (See page 113 for samples from the humorous option.)

- **Film Reel Option (Level 2)**—Put your mouse arrow in the upper left-hand corner and drag diagonally to the right to make a two-framed storyboard. (See page 114 for a sample film reel.)

- **Frames Option (Level 2)**—Choose an animal frame, a curtain frame, or a window frame. Click in the upper left-hand corner and drag to full screen size. Place a picture into the center of the screen.

Writing a Story:

By clicking on the Typewriter tool, you can choose a font from the bottom of the screen, click the mouse on the screen and write. **Note:** There are additional fonts not found in the original *Kid Pix*.

Using Rubber Stamps:

The rubber stamps in KPS are similar to the original stamps in *Kid Pix*, but there is more of a selection, as well as the ability to change stamp positions easily. (See page 115 for the Pick a Stamp Set screen.)

To see all the choices available, select Pick a Stamp Set from the GOODIES menu. Use the down arrow at the right of the selection menu to find more stamps. When you find the picture that you want, double-click on the picture in that set.

Notice the motion commands in the lower left-hand corner. Click on Still to choose not to move the stamp from the original position. Click on Spin to have the stamp rotate in four turns. Click Flip Horizontal to have the stamp flip left and right. Click on Flip Vertical, and the stamp will flip top to bottom. Hold down the shift, option, and command keys to change the sizes of your stamps. Hold down the control and shift keys to change stamp sizes.

Using the Moving Van:

Create your own original picture on your drawing screen or use some of the rubber stamps to create a picture. To move parts of your picture to other places on the screen, you can use the Moving Van tool.

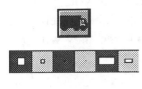

Select the Moving Van tool. Notice the choices at the bottom of the screen. Click on a shape and move your mouse to the screen. Hold down the mouse button and move the mouse. Watch how part of your picture moves in the shape you chose. When you lift your finger off the mouse, the part you moved will stay.

Remember, you can always change the last move you made by selecting The Undo Guy. He will erase the last thing you did. The following methods are some interesting ways of moving your picture around.

Select the Moving Van tool and one of the shapes at the bottom of the screen. Click on part of your picture, hold down the option key, and move the mouse. You have now made a copy of the part that you moved.

There are even more options for the Moving Van. You can adjust the size and part of the picture you want to move by using special options. (See page 116 for the Tool Options screen.)

The Lasso tool will shrink to select the first change in color it touches. Hold down the option key while moving the Lasso with the mouse to select the exact area you have surrounded.

You can paint with the selection you made by holding down the apple and command keys while you move the mouse.

You can paint with the adjustable-size Moving Van by holding down the control and shift keys while you move the mouse.

Using the Eyedropper Tool:

Select the Eyedropper and click on a color in your picture. That color now appears in the color box as the current color. You can use any of the tools, now and they will work in that color.

Using ColorMe, DrawMe, and Hidden Pictures:

Select ColorMe from the GOODIES menu. Here are many pages that can be treated similarly to a coloring book. They can be colored right on the screen and printed or printed and colored later.

Select Hidden Pictures from the GOODIES menu. Choose the eraser tool and the special Hidden Picture eraser. Move the eraser around the screen to reveal as much of the hidden picture as possible. Select Pick Hidden Pictures to swap pictures from another set. When you find the one, you want click OK.

Select DrawMe from the GOODIES menu. Listen to a story segment and see how you can illustrate it. The selections are at random, and you will probably never get the same one twice. You can even erase the words on the screen with one of the erasers. To save the DrawMe picture, select Save a Picture from the FILE menu.

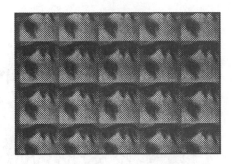

Samples of Rectangles and Squares

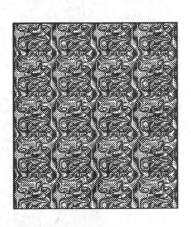

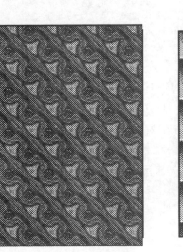

Samples of Circles and Ovals

Samples of Three-Dimensional Pictures

Sample of Bug Frame

      108

Sample of a Bug Frame Enlarged

Sample of a Hand Frame

Samples of Math Problems

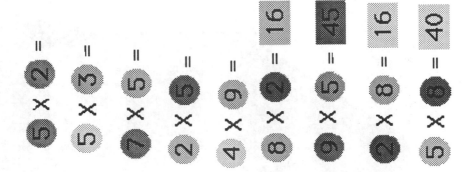

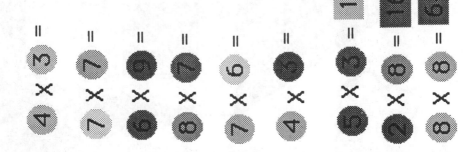

Sample Picture of a House

Samples from the Humorous Option

Sample Film Reel

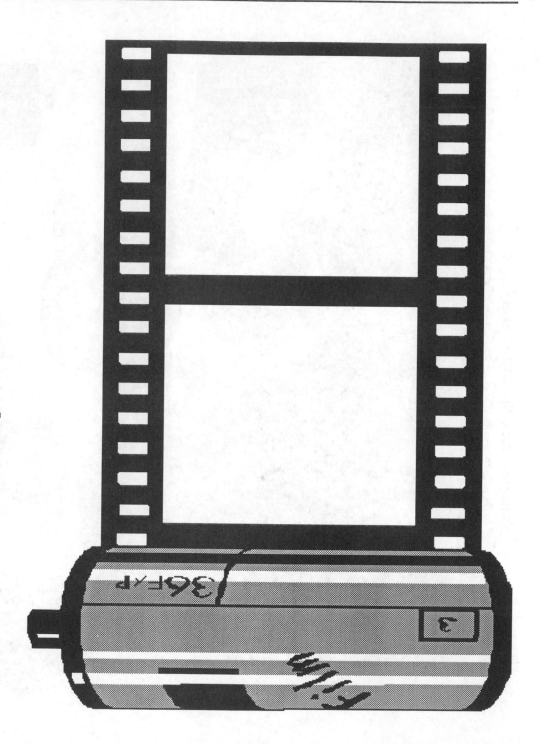

Pick a Stamp Set Screen

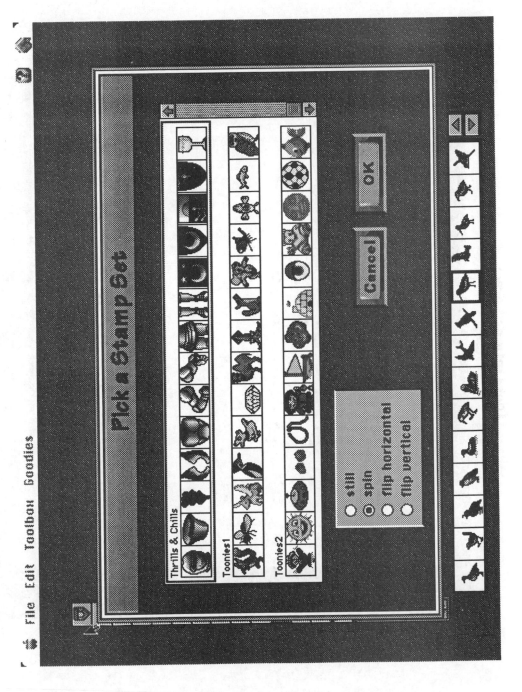

Tool Options Screen

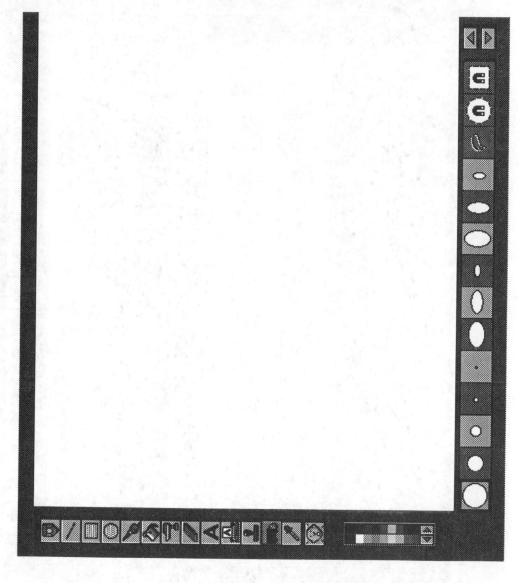

Exploring Moopies:

Moopies entice you to explore new tool options, including animated pictures to produce animated projects. Follow along, and you will learn and enjoy becoming an animator. To start the Moopies project, double-click on Moopies in the *Kid Pix Studio* menu.

Choosing a Background and Adding Dimension:

Select Pick a Background! from the GOODIES menu. If you click on the right arrow at the middle of the screen, you can move backgrounds across the screen. The background that is under the red arrows in the middle of the screen will go to the Moopie screen when you click OK. Notice that there is also a choice to use pictures from a CD. (See page 122 for the Pick a Background screen.)

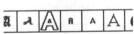

Choose a background picture. Select the Typewriter tool. Choose a font from the bottom of the screen. Click where you want your words to be and write. You can use any of the tools that are shown on the left tool menu. Try using the wacky pencil to draw parts of your picture. After you have tried several tools, clear your screen.

Using Toonies1 or Toonies2 or Watch the Stamps Jump:

Click on the Rubber Stamp tool. Then, select Pick a Stamp Set from the GOODIES menu. Click on the bottom arrow until the Toonies1 and Toonies2 sets show. (See page 123 for the Pick a Stamp Set screen.)

Choose various stamps to see how they work. Select Wacky Brush and notice that the bottom of the screen has options that were not there before. (See page 124 for samples of the Wacky Brush option.)

Hold down the shift, option, and command keys to change the sizes of your stamps. Hold down the control and shift keys to change stamp sizes.

Now clear your screen, and you will put together a moving picture with music.

Select Pick a Stamp Set from the GOODIES menu. Move the arrow down to Toonies1, and click on the girl's skirt, and then click on the drawing screen. Now add her blouse and her head. Choose the stamps to make the boy. Add a balloon and a party hat. Add more stamps to your creation.

Select the Typewriter tool and a font to add writing to your picture. Next add sound to your picture. Select Pick a Sound from the GOODIES menu. Move the right arrow until the sound you like appears under the red arrows in the middle of the screen. You can preview your sound by clicking on Preview Sound. Select the timing of your sound. **Note:** Select the playing time for your sound so it does not play all the time. (See page 125 for the Pick a Sound screen.)

You can also record your own sound by clicking on the microphone icon.

Saving a Moopie:

You can save your Moopie in several different ways. Select Save a Moopie from the FILE menu. It will now be saved in a Moopies file that you can open up and edit in Moopies. If you want to save your Moopies for use in a slide show, select Save for Slide Show. (See pages 126 and 127 for what you can do with Moopies.)

Exploring the Stampimator:

Stampimator lets you pick a background, add stamps that you direct to move on the screen with musical accompaniment, and add animated pictures to produce animated projects. Follow along, and you will learn about and enjoy becoming an animator.

To start the Stampimator project, double-click on Stampimator in the *Kid Pix Studio* menu. Select Pick a Background from the GOODIES menu. Click OK to select a background. (See page 128 for how to pick a background.)

Choosing a Background and Adding Dimension:

Select Pick a Background from the GOODIES menu. If you click on the right arrow at the middle of the screen, you move backgrounds across the screen. The background that is under the red arrows in the middle of the screen will go to the Stampimator screen when you click OK. Notice that there is a choice to use pictures from a CD. (See page 129 for sample of a background.)

Animating the Rubber Stamps:

Click on the Rubber Stamp tool. Select Pick a Stamp Set from the GOODIES menu. Click on the bottom arrow until the stamp set you want appears. Click OK and choose a stamp from that set for your picture. Click on the cast box. Your choice appears in the box. Click on a spot in the picture to start a path. Move your mouse across the screen to make the path. You can move in circles or up and down. The stamp moves with you. There can be up to four actors in your movie.

Carefully follow the directions below for an animated show.

- Click on the Rubber Stamp tool.
- Click on the first cast box.
- Click on a Rubber Stamp (it appears in the cast box).
- Click on a point on the screen and move it along a path.
- The bar at the top fills with red, showing the time used.
- Start with another stamp by clicking on the second cast box and selecting another Rubber Stamp.

Choose various stamps to see how they work. Select Wacky Brush and notice that the bottom of the screen has options that were not there before.

Saving a Stampimator:

You can save your Stampimator in several different ways. Select Save a Stampimator from the FILE menu. It will now be saved in a Stampimator file that you can open up and edit in Stampimator. If you want the save your Stampimator for use in a slide show, select Save for SlideShow.

Exploring Digital Puppets:

The Digital Puppets Project turns you into a puppet master who uses a computer to control the puppets. Select Digital Puppets from the *Kid Pix Studio* menu and get ready for the creation of a puppet show.

To start your puppet production, choose Digital Puppets from the *Kid Pix Studio* main menu.

There are two ways to select your puppet. You automatically see a puppet when you choose Digital Puppets, or you can go to the GOODIES menu and select Pick a Puppet. Select a puppet and then click OK.

Now comes the creative part of the production. Movement of your puppet is created by using the numbers, letters, and arrow keys on the keyboard. Mouth movements are created by using the bottom row of keyboard keys. Type in your name and watch the puppet move. Type in the spelling words of the week and watch the movement. Add music by selecting Pick a Sound from the GOODIES menu. Add a background to your production by selecting Pick a Background from the GOODIES menu.

Saving a Digital Puppet:

You can save your Digital Puppet in several different ways. Select Save a Digital Puppet from the FILE menu. It will now be saved in a Digital Puppet file that you can open up and edit in Digital Puppet. If you want to save your Digital Puppet for use in a slide show, select Save for SlideShow, and it will be saved as a movie to add to a Slide Show project.

Pick a Background Screen

Pick a Stamp Set Screen

Samples of the Wacky Brush Option

Pick a Sound Screen

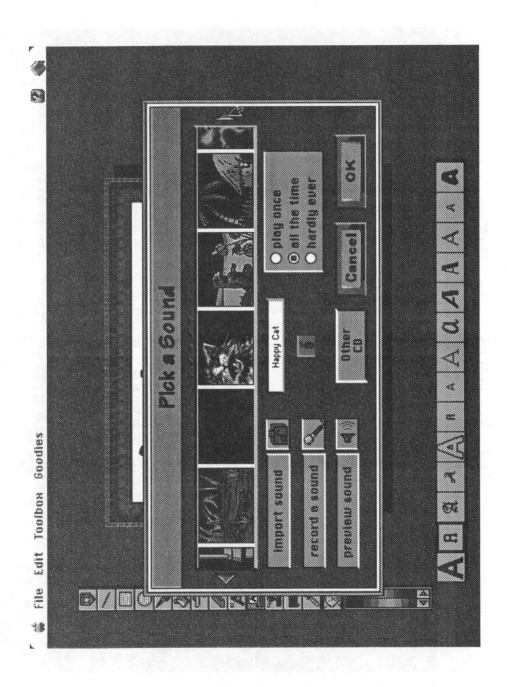

What You Can Do with Moopies

What You Can Do with Moopies

How to Pick a Background

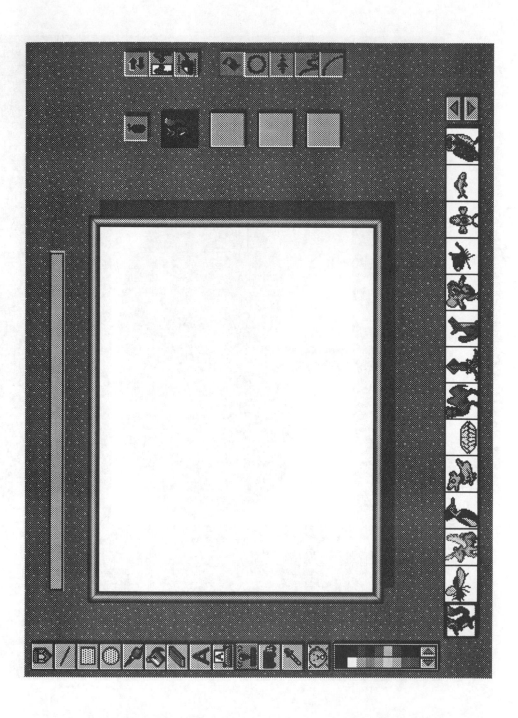

A Sample of a Background

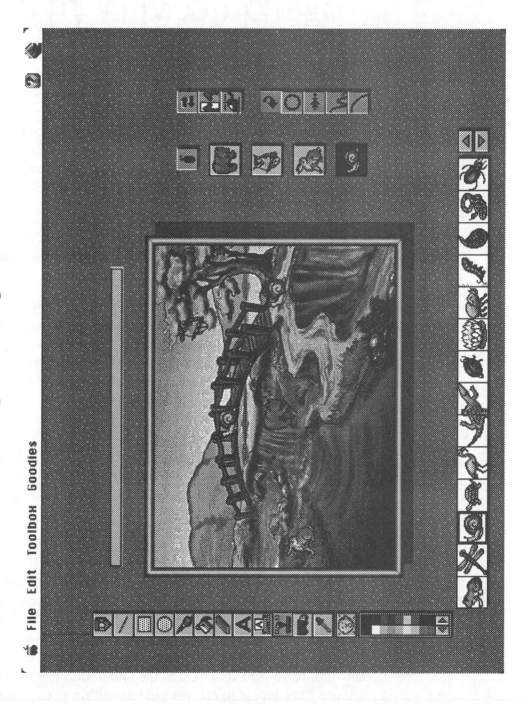

Using Wacky TV in KP and KPS

The Wacky TV option is an on-screen movie player which allows you to import movies into your *Kid Pix* pictures. *Kid Pix Studio* for Windows plays and saves movies in the AVI format only. The Macintosh version plays and saves only as QuickTime movies.

Kid Pix Studio contains more than 100 already made Wacky TV movies, but it can also use movies that you make. You can use Moopies, Stampimations, and Digital Puppet Shows that you have saved for SlideShow.

If you are using *Kid Pix*, the Wacky TV segments can be copied and pasted into any *Kid Pix* picture. You can match the color of the background in the TV segment by using the Paint Can tool. When you are ready, select Play Movie from the SWITCHEROO menu to start the animation. Click on the screen to stop the animation.

Moving Wacky TV Onto Your Screen

You can start the Wacky TV by choosing it in the Project Picker on the main menu or by choosing Pick a Movie from the GOODIES menu in *Kid Pix*. The Wacky TV appears on the screen. Choose one of the movies listed on the screen. (See pages 131 and 132 for examples.)

If you got to Wacky TV using Pick a Movie from the GOODIES menu in *Kid Pix*, click on the Paste Jar icon to paste your Wacky TV picture into the *Kid Pix* screen. A freeze frame of your movie appears on the screen with a Paste Jar stuck to it. Move your mouse to where you want the movie to appear. Click the mouse once to paste your movie into your picture. Go to the GOODIES menu and choose Play Movie to run your movie within your picture.

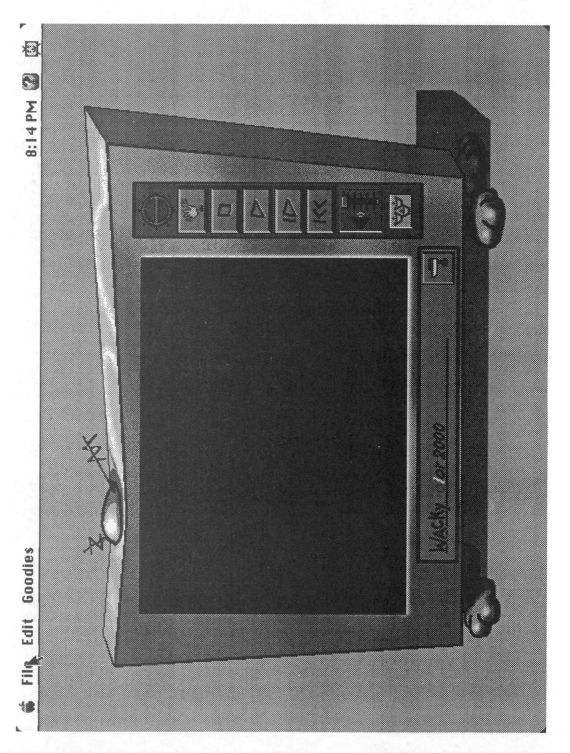

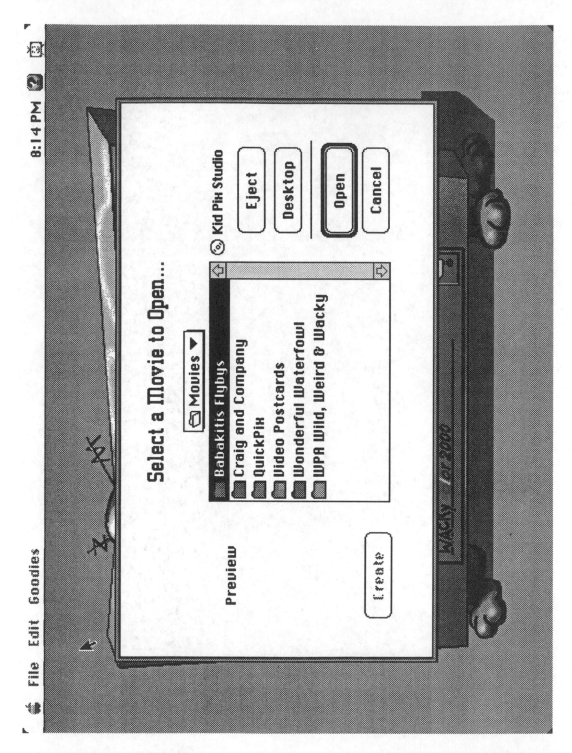

Student Projects Index

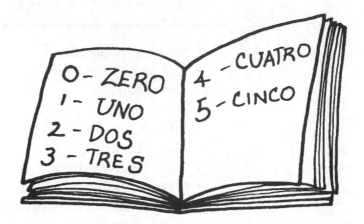

Spanish Number Book

InfoNet: One of the ways that a new language is learned is by writing the language and visualizing that language. The Spanish language is spoken in many countries around the world—Spain, South America, Mexico, Central America, Puerto Rico, Cuba, and in many parts of the United States.

This Project: You are going to make a number book in Spanish, which will help you learn the Spanish names for the numbers.

1. Divide the screen into four sections. Select the Line tool and hold down the shift key while you are drawing your lines.

2. Now you need to switch to Spanish. In KP select Switch to Spanish from the GOODIES menu and in KPS select Switch to Spanish from the TOOLBOX menu. Notice that the menu items are all in Spanish now. This will help you to learn Spanish.

3. Select the Text tool from the toolbar.

4. Notice that the alphabet is now in Spanish. When you click on a letter or number, the letter and/or number name will be said in Spanish. This, too, helps in learning a new language.

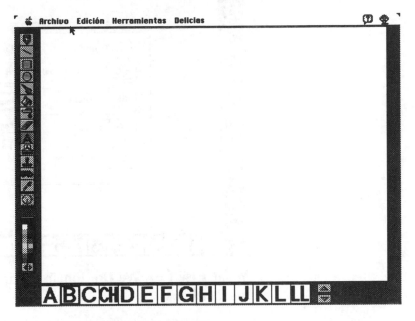

5. Scroll through the alphabet until you come to the numbers. Select 0 and place it on the screen in the upper left-hand box. Choose the letters that spell ZERO. Place each one in the box. You don't need to put a picture in this box.

6. Select the number 1 and place it in the right-hand box. Write the Spanish word UNO. Now place a picture of one item in the box.

7. Continue writing the words and putting in the correct pictures.

0–ZERO	1–UNO	2–DOS
3–TRES	4–CUATRO	

8. Save and print. Select Guardar in the
   ARCHIVO menu.

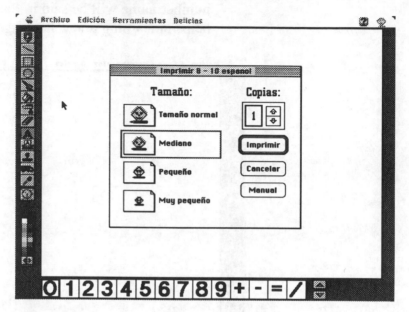

What Else Can We Do: Finish making your Spanish
number book.

1. Divide the drawing screen into four segments again.

2. Continue placing numbers and number words in
   the boxes.

5-CINCO	6–SEIS	7–SIETE
8–OCHO	9–NUEVE	10–DIEZ

3. Print out the pages and assemble them into a book.

4. Import your saved screens into the Slide Show. You
   may want to make a screen title called "Numeros en
   Español", for example.

ZERO

0

UNO

1

DOS

2

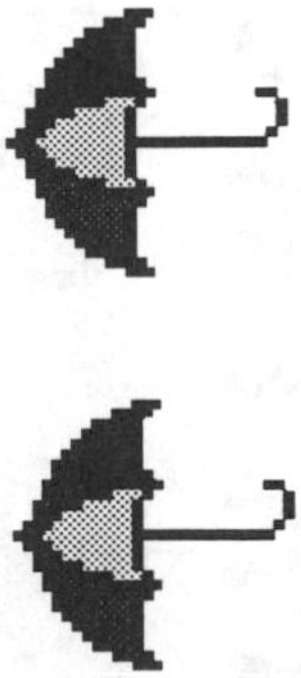

TRES

3

CINCO

5

SEITE

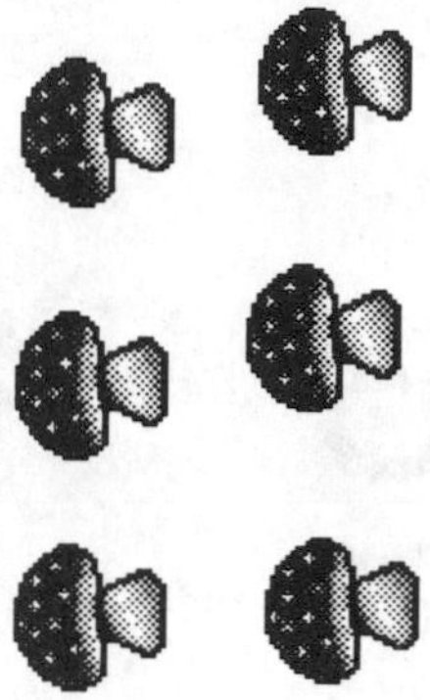

7

CUATRO

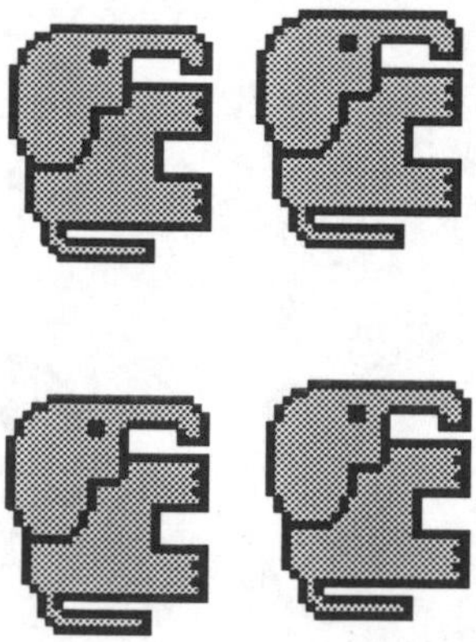

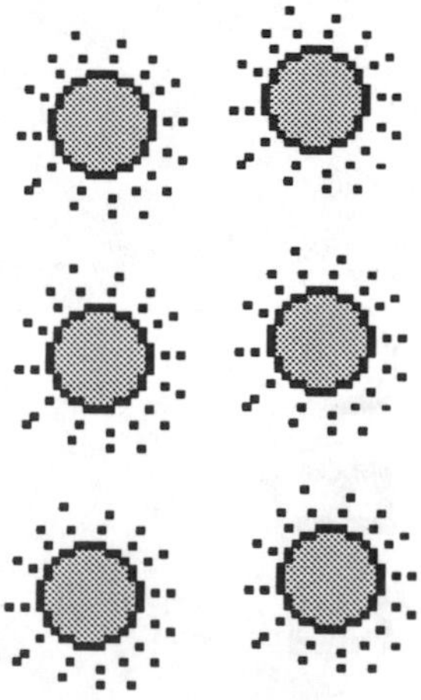

4

SEIS

6

NUEVE

9

OCHO

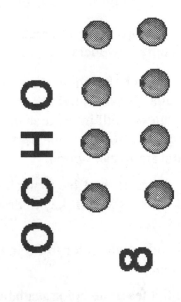

8

0 1 2 3 4
5 6 7 8 9
10
¡NUMEROS!

DIEZ

10

Life on the Seashore

InfoNet: The planet earth looks blue when viewed from outer space because three-fourths of the earth is covered in water. There are three major oceans and many seas which connect to form one world ocean. The seashore may contain mud, sand, and/or rock. Each part of the seashore has its own special types of animals, and some of those animals live in all three parts of the seashore. The animals on the seashore must adapt to living on water and on land.

This Project: In this project you are going to create a seashore habitat with all its animal dwellers.

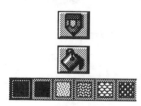

1. Use the Wacky Pencil and light brown to draw the shoreline. Select the Paint Can tool, light brown, and the sandy looking fill pattern. Fill in the area that should be sandy. You could also add some depth to the sandy area, using the spray can option.

2. To draw the horizon line, select the Line tool, choose the color blue, and hold down the shift key to draw a line across the screen.

3. Use the Paint Can tool and a light color to fill in the area that will be the water.

4. Fill in the sky with the lightest blue color available.

5. Use the Wacky Pencil and the color white to draw in waves along the horizon line and in the water.

What Else Can We Do: Adding the shoreline sea creatures and vegetation will complete the depiction of life on the seashore.

1. Now it is time to place the appropriate sea animals into your picture. Select the Rubber Stamp tool and look through the choices of animals and vegetation that you may want to use in your picture.

2. Use the Wacky Pencil tool to draw in any pictures that you cannot find.

3. To title your picture, select the Typewriter tool in KPS, or in KP select the Alphabet Text tool from the GOODIES menu.

4. Save and print your picture. You may want to use this picture as a cover to a report on oceanography.

5. This could be the first slide in a slide show on sea life. The other slides might feature some of the sea animals you used in your seashore picture, with information about each animal on the slide.

6. If you have recording capabilities, use the 32 seconds and have your friends help you with making sea sounds, or you could play part of a tape that has sea shanties or sea sounds on it.

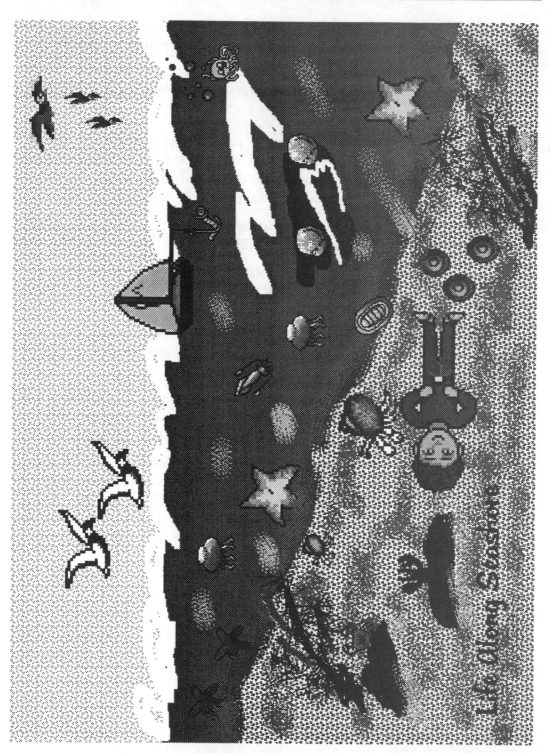

Travel Brochure

InfoNet: When people are deciding where to take a vacation, they may consult with a travel agent, and/or read brochures about potential vacation places. These brochures are created to attract those tourists. Tourism is a great source of income to many countries.

This Project: You are going to create a travel brochure that would entice someone to plan a vacation in your area. You will need to find out some information about the place that you choose.

1. Research the area that you have chosen:

   - Location and history
   - Things to buy that are unique
   - Places of interest
   - Map of the area
   - Special foods
   - Transportation
   - Manner of dress
   - Types of recreation

2. This brochure is going to be a trifold. A trifold has six sides. You will divide the first screen into three sections and design each individual section. After printing the first page, you will then do the same thing on the second page. After both pages are printed, cut them apart and glue them onto a piece of construction paper to complete your brochure.

3. Divide the screen into thirds. Select the Line tool, hold down the shift key, and divide the screen.

4. The section on the far left will be your cover. Use the Type Text tool from the GOODIES menu in KP. If you are using KPS, select the Typewriter tool. Type in an inviting phrase to make people want to read the rest of your brochure.

5. Add a graphic by using the Rubber Stamp tool and options; that will help illustrate your place.

6. The middle section is for showing things that you can do in the place that you are telling about. Title this section "Things to Do."

7. Using the Rubber Stamp tool, select some options that will help show the things that you can do.

8. The final panel is to show the places that tourists can go visit while on vacation. Title this section "Places to Go." Now add graphics to show some of these places to go.

9. Save your work and print your page.

10. Fold a piece of construction paper into thirds.

11. Cut your page along the solid line. You now have three panels for your brochure. Glue the Cover, Things to Do page and the Places to Go page. You now have one half of the brochure completed.

12. Clear your screen and follow the directions in #1.

13. Label the first section "Location and History." Include information about the location and history of your vacation place.

14. On the middle section, explain why your vacation place is a fun place to visit.

15. On the last section, tell your potential customers where and how they can arrange for their trip.

16. Print your page. Cut apart your three sections and place them on a piece of construction paper which has been in thirds.

Places To Do

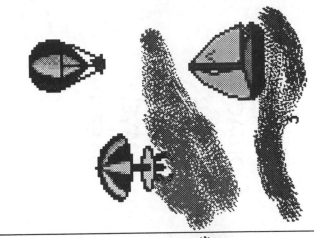

Things to Do

OLE!

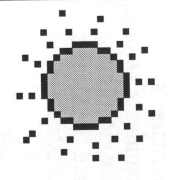

Visit Sunny Spain

CONTACT YOUR LOCAL TRAVEL AGENT

Barbara Berry
555-1234

6

Spain

A FUN PLACE TO VISIT

5

LOCATION

Spain occupies a peninsula between the mountains and the Straits of Gibralter

4

Print Projects

InfoNet: It is nice to give handmade gifts on special occasions. Making a gift with the computer makes it extra special for the receiver of the gift. It shows how really creative and high tech you are.

This Project: You are going to make personalized stationery as a gift for a friend. You will need to know the name and address of the person who will be receiving your gift.

1. To make the border for the stationery, select the Wacky Pencil tool, a color, and a thick line width. Hold your mouse as steady as possible as you go down both sides and across the top and bottom of your computer screen. Stay as close to the black lines on the screen as possible. Remember: You can use the Undo Guy or the Eraser tool to remove any mistakes.

2. Select the Wacky Brush tool and an option that you can use to draw over the border. (See page 150 for an example of a stationery border.)

3. Next you will need to make the heading for the personalized stationery. Select Type Text from the GOODIES menu in KP, or the Typewriter tool in KPS. Choose a font that you like.

4. Click at the top middle of the screen and type in the name, address, and phone number of the person who will be receiving this stationery. (See page 151 for an example of a stationery card.)

5. Print your stationery. To print more than one piece of stationery, click on the up arrow under Copies:.

What Else Can We Do: Try some other types of printing projects that you can use as gifts, invitations, and/or gift tags.

1. Make a recipe card by drawing a border and adding lines across the page so that a recipe can be written out. You may also want to add clip art to your recipe card. (See page 152 for an example of a recipe card.)

2. Make party invitations. (See page 153 for an example of a party invitation.)

3. Make gift tags and labels. Print these out in smaller sizes. (See page 154 for an example of gift tags and labels.)

Example of Stationery Border

Example of Stationery Card

Mary Lopez
345 Mulberry Lane
Harmony, CA 67805

Example of a Recipe Card

Recipe

Example of a Party Invitation

Who: Mary Smith

When: 3/23/97

Where: 123 Pine St.

Why: It's My **Birthday!**

Mary

R.S.V.P. 555-1234

Come to My Party!

Example of Gift Tags and Labels

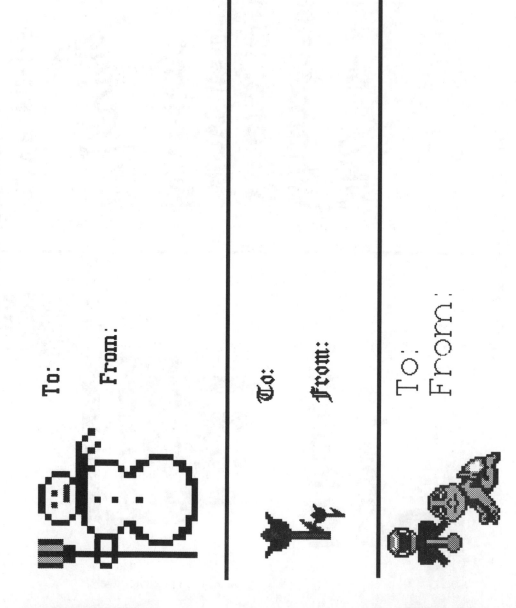

Picture a Fraction

InfoNet: Fractions are all around us. When you buy a pizza, it is usually divided into eight pieces, which means that you get one-eighth of the pizza when you take a slice. An hour is divided into 60 minutes, which means that each minute is one-sixtieth of an hour. If you buy a dozen doughnuts and take one doughnut, you are taking one-twelfth of the dozen doughnuts.

This Project: You are going to illustrate various fraction problems.

1. There are four members in your family. A pizza delivery person brings a pizza that has not been cut. Each family member will get one piece of pizza that is the same size as everyone else's. Show how you will divide the pizza equally.

2. Use the Oval tool and hold down the shift key to make a perfectly round pizza.

3. Use the Line tool to divide up the pizza.

4. Use the Rubber Stamp tool and options to put goodies on your pizza.

5. If you are using KP, select Type Text from the GOODIES menu to write the problem. If you are using KPS, select the Typewriter tool.

6. Print your fraction story problem and illustration.

What Else Can We Do: Now choose one of the problems below and illustrate the solution.

1. You have a dozen cookies and want to give each friend the same number. Show how the cookies would be divided. What fraction would each friend have?

2. Alex brought ten strawberries to school and wants to give each teacher one-tenth of the strawberries. Show how many strawberries each teacher would get. You can use the Rubber Stamp tool, the strawberry option, and the Wacky Pencil to show your problem.

3. For the classroom picnic your teacher asked you to bring one-half hamburger sandwiches and one-half hot dogs. Show how many you would bring of each sandwich.

4. Tom and Anita go to a Chinese restaurant. They are going to each have one-half a bowl of rice.

5. Mary's mom gave her a party. Mary's five best friends came to the party. Each one wanted an equal part of the cake. Show how the cake was divided into five parts.

The pizza has to be divided into four equal parts to feed the family of four.

Marian

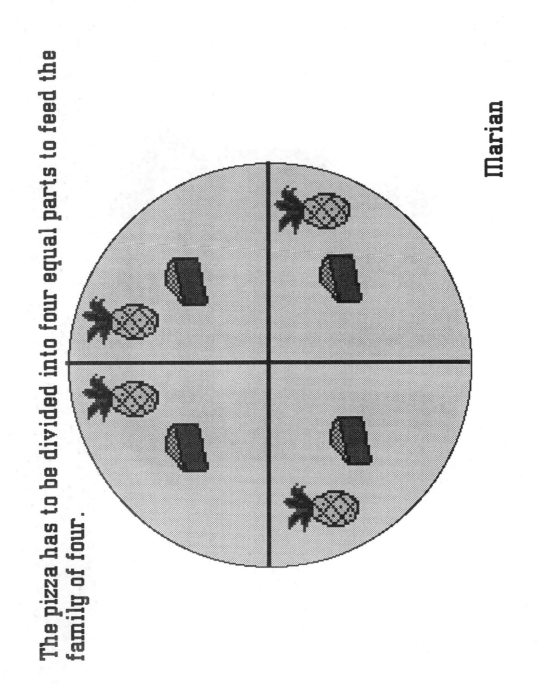

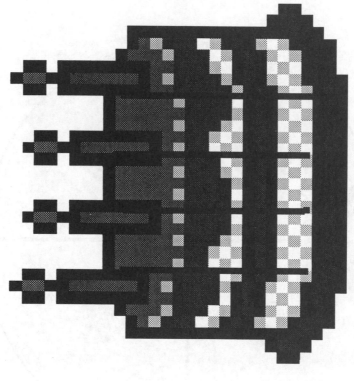

Divide the cake into five parts

Morse Code

InfoNet: Long before computers and the Internet were invented, people were sending messages to each other by code. The most famous code was developed by Samuel Morse in the 1830s. Each letter of the alphabet was given a combination of long and short taps called dashes and dots. These were transmitted across the country on telegraph wires similar to today's telephone lines. People went to a telegraph office to send messages because there were no phones then.

This Project: You are going to make your own copy of Morse code and then write a coded message to a friend to decipher.

1. Divide the screen into three parts by using the Line tool and holding the shift key down as you make the line.

2. To write the English or Spanish alphabet on the screen, select the Text tool from the tool menu. Click on a letter and then click on the screen where you want it to be.

3. Put the letters A through I in the first column on the left.

4. Put the letters J through R in the middle column.

5. Put the letters S through Z in the last column.

6. Copy the code for each letter carefully. Use the period key and the hyphen key for the dots and dashes. (See page 161 for a copy of the Morse code.)

7. Print out your Morse code.

What Else Can We Do: Use your Morse code paper to decipher the following messages. After you have deciphered all of these messages, send a Morse code message to a friend.

1. (... --- ...)

    (__ __ __)

2. (... -- .. .-.. .)

    (__ __ __ __ __)

3. (--. --- --- -.. ..-. --- .-. -.-- --- ..-)

    (__ __ __ __ __ __ __ __ __ __)

4. (--. --- --- -.. -... -.-- .)

    (__ __ __ __ __ __ __)

Morse Code

A ._	**J** .___	**S** ...	
B _...	**K** _._	**T** _	
C _._.	**L** ._..	**U** .._	
D _..	**M** __	**V** ..._	
E .	**N** _.	**W** .__	
F .._.	**O** ___	**X** _.._	
G __.	**P** .__.	**Y** _.__	
H	**Q** __._	**Z** __..	
I ..	**R** ._.		

Butterfly Note Holder

InfoNet: Butterflies wings have exactly the same symmetrical design. They have antennas growing out of their heads and bodies to which the wings are attached.

This Project: In this project you are going to make a butterfly with both wings matching in design and then glue them onto a clothespin that can be used as a note holder.

1. To draw the outline of the butterfly, select the Wacky Brush tool and the three-dimensional option.

2. Make an x across the screen with the Wacky Brush and the three-dimensional option. Connect the ends of the x to form the wings of the butterfly.

3. Use the Wacky Brush tool to also draw the body.

4. To make the head, select the Oval tool and the empty box option and draw in the head at the top of the body.

5. To fill the body and wings with color, select the Paint Can tool, any color, and patterns from the options menu. Be sure to match both wings with the same patterns and colors.

6. To make the designs, select the Wacky Brush tool and the magnifying glass option.

7. Move the mouse to the right wing and click. Notice how the pattern is magnified. Now do it on the left wing in the same place so that it matches.

What Else Can We Do: You can add colors to the magnified areas to finish your butterfly.

1. Select the Paint Can tool, any color, and click in an empty space in the magnified circle.

2. Make the colors match on both sides.

3. Try other options in the Wacky Brush options to add decorations to the wings. Make sure that whatever you do to one wing, you match it to the other wing.

4. Print your butterfly small enough to fit on the clothespin.

5. Cut out your butterfly and glue it onto a clothespin.

6. You may want to paste your butterfly onto heavier paper before gluing it to the clothespin.

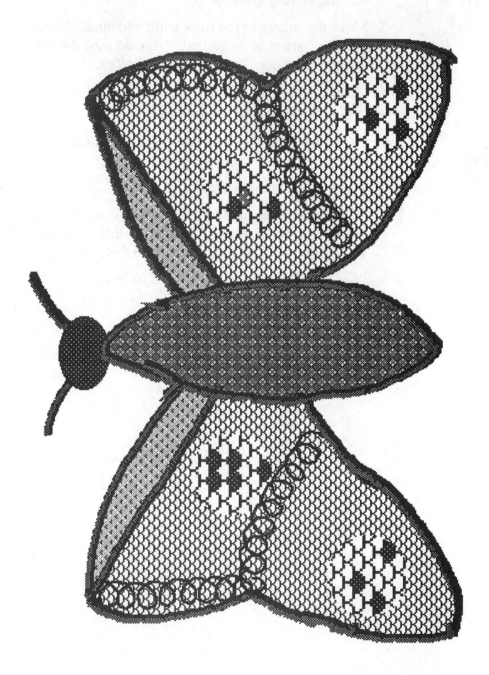

Make a Family Quilt

InfoNet: Quilts have been made from the time pioneers first came to the United States. Shapes are cut and sewn together to make one large rectangle. Originally the quilts were made from fabric with a layer of cotton or wool and a piece of cloth as the backing. Tiny stitches were sewn on many different designs to finish the quilt.

This Project: You are going to design a quilt, using art work that tells something about your family. The tiny stitches that the pioneers used will be duplicated by using the Wacky Brush tool.

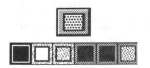

1. To make the base of the quilt, you need to draw a large square on the screen. Select the Rectangle tool and the empty box option. Click on the screen and while holding the shift key down, pull diagonally.

2. To make the inside of the quilt, click on any color and a pattern. Pull diagonally to make the pieces of the quilt. If you don't want borders around the pieces of your quilt, hold down the option or control key as you draw. (See page 167 for an example of how to make the pieces of your quilt.)

3. Fill the quilt with squares or rectangles. If some of the pieces don't touch each other, when you are finished drawing the pieces, select the Paint Can tool, any color, and click on an empty space and watch the quilt fill with color. (See page 168 for an example of this step.)

What Else Can We Do: Now you can add pictures of things that your family likes to do together.

1. Select the Rubber Stamp tool and look through the options to find stamps that show things related to your family. What kinds of foods, sports, games, travel, and/or hobbies do the members of your family like? Put in the stamps to illustrate their likes. (See page 169 for an example of family likes.)

2. Now you need to title your quilt. Select the Type Text from the GOODIES menu in KP, or select the Typewriter tool in KPS. Click on the screen where you want your writing to start.

3. Type in your family name.

4. To sew the pieces of fabric together, use the Wacky Brush tool and the zigzag option and move your mouse around the fabric pieces. (See page 170 for an example of this.)

5. Print your quilt. (See page 171 for an example of a finished quilt.) You can also make a quilt representing your state. Use steps one to three and choose pictures that represent your state to stamp on the fabric. (See page 172 for a sample of a state quilt.)

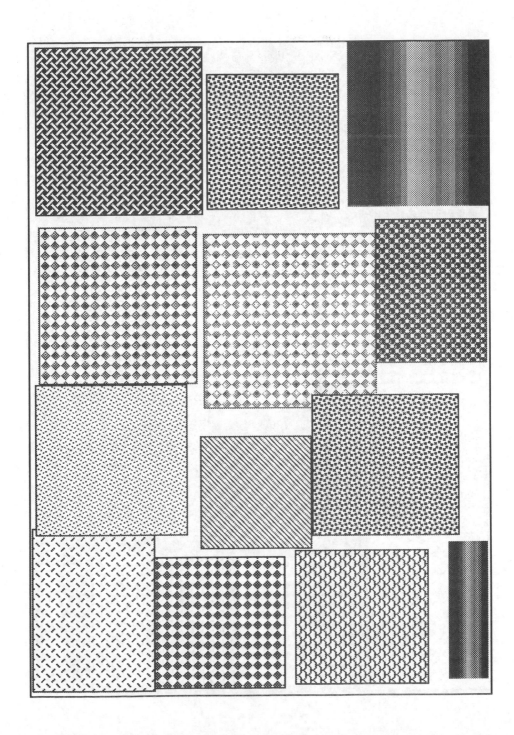

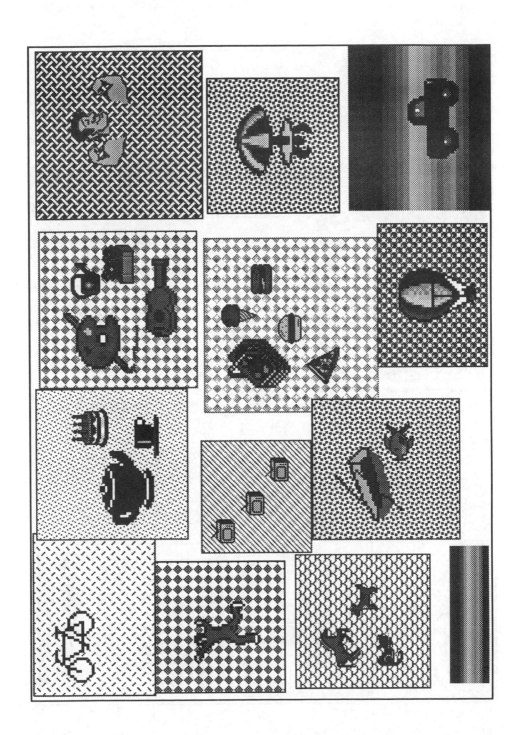

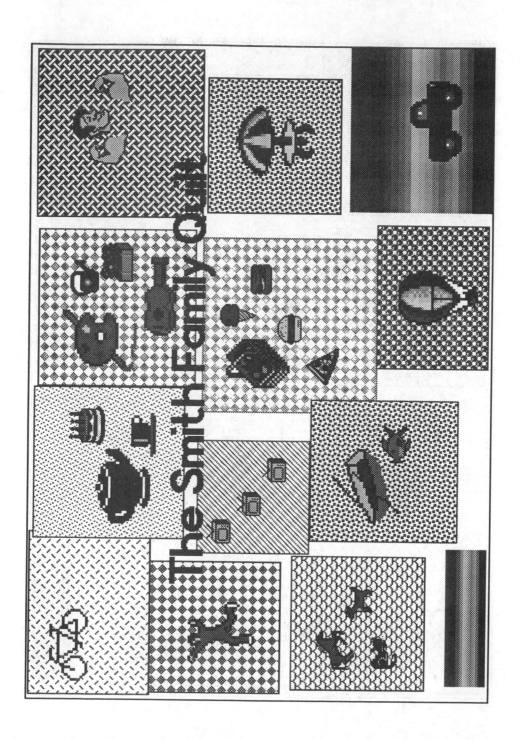

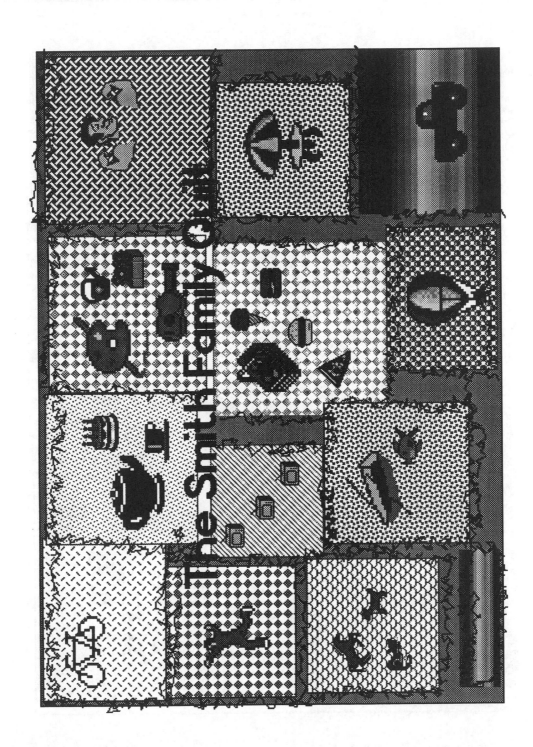

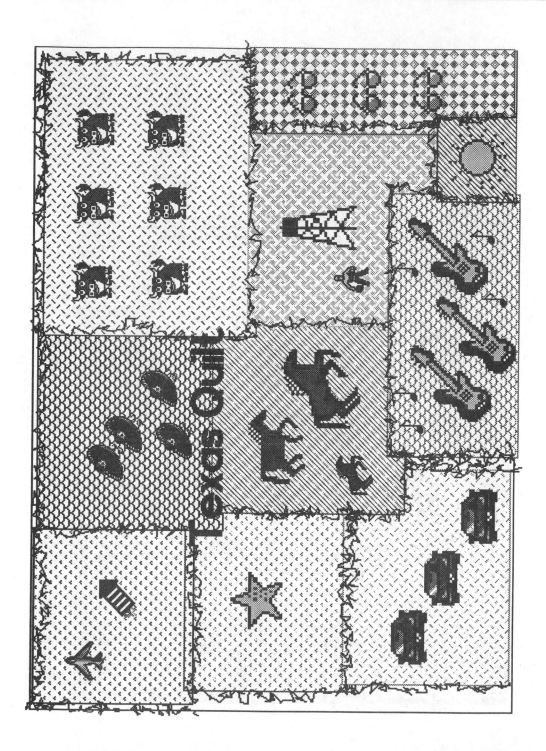

Native American Totem Pole

InfoNet: Native Americans living in the Pacific Northwest carved totems that depicted the bodies of animals and other figures. The poles were made to protect the Native Americans from harm. They were constructed from cedar trees whose bark had been removed. Native Americans used chisels to carve the figures on their poles. Today the tribal elders teach young tribal members to carve figures to record and remember their history.

This Project: You are going to carve a totem on the drawing screen, instead of using a chisel.

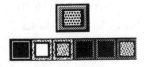

1. Select the Rectangle tool, the color brown, and the filled box option.

2. Holding the mouse button down and pulling diagonally, make a long rectangle on the drawing screen.

3. To put figures on your totem, select the Rubber Stamp tool and place the figures on the rectangle. (See page 175 for an example of figures on a rectangle.)

4. Now it is time to carve your totem. Select the Eraser tool and one of the four erasers on the left of the option bar.

5. Hold down your mouse button as you carve around the figures that you stamped.

What Else Can We Do: Now that your totem is carved, place it in an appropriate setting. The Pacific Northwest is an area of dense forests; therefore, placing trees around your totem will make it more authentic.

1. Select the Rubber Stamp tool and find appropriate stamps to place in your drawing.

2. To make a horizon line in your picture, select the Line tool, and the color blue and draw across the picture. Be sure that there is no break in the line. If there is a break, then the color will run all over the screen. If this happens, use the Undo Guy and the Wacky Pencil tool to close the line.

3. Select the Paint Can tool, and the color blue and click above the horizon line to fill in the screen with blue sky. Use a light brown color and fill in the ground area. (See page 176 for an example of a totem pole set in an authentic scene.)

4. Print your picture. You can cut out your totem and glue it to an empty towel roll. You may want to use this picture as the cover to a report on Northwestern Native Americans. Or, you may want to use this as part of a slide show.

Zoo Habitat

InfoNet: Zoos throughout the world are constructing living areas that resemble the natural habitats of the animals they house. No longer are animals being kept in cages, but they are allowed to roam in habitats that closely resemble their native territories. There are four basic habitats: desert, water, polar, and forest.

This Project: In this project you will construct a zoo that uses natural habitats for its animals.

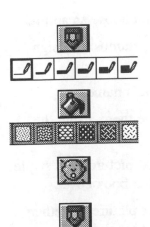

1. Select the Wacky Pencil tool and the medium width line to draw an outline for the pathway that goes from the left to the right side of the drawing screen.

2. To make the pathway look like stones, select the Paint Can tool and a fill that looks like pebbles. Click on the pathway and watch it fill with pebbles. If you don't like how it looks, select the Undo Guy tool.

3. Draw rocks for the habitats with the Wacky Pencil tool and use some interesting fills with the Paint Can tool.

4. You will need to decide which animals you want to place in your zoo.

5. Create areas in your picture that are similar to the ones where the animals live naturally. Do you need any of the following:

- trees
- plants
- desert areas
- sand
- water areas
- grassy areas

6. Select the Rubber Stamp tool and choose your zoo animals.

7. Place them in the areas that are similar to where they live. Do several animals need the same type of habitat?

8. Select the Wacky Brush tool and choose the options to make grass and sandy areas.

9. Save your picture, using the title (Zoo Habitat:your initials) and then print your work.

What Else Can We Do: Now you are going to add more screens showing the individual habitats for each animal. Our first picture, Zoo Habitat, can be the cover of a book or the first slide in an animal slide show.

1. Select the Rubber Stamp tool and choose an animal.

2. Use the drawing tools and rubber stamps to design the habitat of the animal.

3. Save this picture, using the animal's name.

4. Design two more screens and save them, using the animals' names.

5. Print out your three animal habitat pictures and staple them together with the Zoo Habitat book cover.

6. Select SlideShow and put all your pictures together with the Zoo Habitat page as the first slide.

7. You may want to have your friends help you record the appropriate sounds for each animal picture.

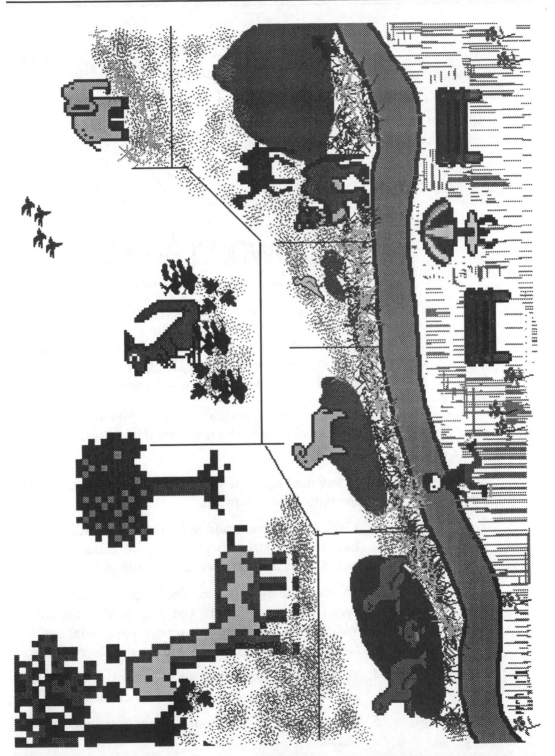

Clowning Around

InfoNet: Clowns have been making people laugh for centuries. They were called jesters in the middle ages and traveled around the country making people laugh. Clowns appear in the circus where they perform tricks, jokes, and do antics to bring laughter to the audience.

This Project: By using various shapes, you are going to make your own clown which will then be turned into a puppet.

1. Select the Oval tool and the empty box option from the bottom screen menu.

2. Click on the screen and pull diagonally until you have the face size that you want. To make the face round, hold down the shift key while pulling.

3. To make the eyes, use the Oval tool and draw in the eyes size that you want. You may want to use the Wacky Pencil tool to draw unique eyes. Making facial features larger often adds to the clown's look.

4. To make the nose, select the Oval tool, the color red, and the filled box option. Draw in the nose.

5. Use the Wacky Pencil tool to draw in the mouth and ears.

6. To make the hat, use the Line tool.

7. Decorate the hat, using any of the tools and options that you like.

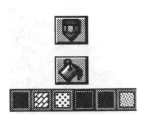

8. To make the ruffled collar, draw it with the Wacky Pencil tool.

9. Use the Wacky Pencil tool to draw in the costume. Use the Paint Can tool and several different colors and patterns to fill in the costume.

10. Save and then Print your clown. (See page 182 for an example of a clown.)

What Else Can We Do: You are going to make your clown into a puppet by enlarging the parts and putting each part on a separate screen.

1. Use the Oval tool and the empty box option to draw a large circle for your clown face. Remember to save room for your clown's hat. Fill the screen with the face and hat.

2. Make the hat the same way that you did the first time.

3. Make the eyes, nose, and mouth the same way.

4. Save this picture, naming it (clown face:your initials) and then print it.

5. Clear your screen.

6. Use the Wacky Pencil tool to draw the costume. You need to make the costume almost as large as the screen. Decorate the costume.

7. Save this using the name (clown body:your initials).

8. Print your clown body.

9. Cut out the face and the body and glue them onto a paper bag to make a puppet. (See page 183 for an example of a clown puppet.)

Example of a Clown

Example of a Clown Puppet

I Think I Can!

InfoNet: The famous children's story *The Little Engine That Could* by Watty Piper tells the story of an engine that never gave up against strong odds.

This Project: In this project you are going to illustrate the famous story of *The Little Engine That Could*.

1. Select the Wacky Pencil tool, the color brown, and the small line width.

2. Start at the very bottom of the screen and draw a mountain. Be sure that both the beginning and ending points of the line touch the bottom of the screen.

3. Select the Paint Can tool and click in the middle of your mountain to fill it with color.

4. Remember you can erase your last move by clicking on the Undo Guy.

5. Select the Rubber Stamp tool. Then select Swap Stamps and the Transportation choices from the SWITCHEROO menu.

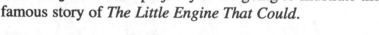

6. Find the stamp of the engine, click, and then hold down the option key while you click where you want the engine on the screen.

7. Click on the other railroad cars that you want as part of your train.

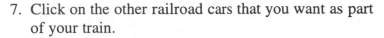

8. To make the railroad tracks, select the Straight Line tool, choose black, and hold down the shift key as you make your tracks.

What Else Can We Do: Now you will complete your picture by adding rubber stamps and text.

1. Select the Rubber Stamp tool and choose trees, flowers, and animals for your picture.

2. To make snow at the top of the mountain, select the Wacky Brush tool and choose the spray can option. Select white and spray the top of the mountain.

3. To make a river, select the Wacky Pencil tool, the color blue, and the medium width. Draw in your river.

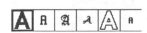

4. To make the puffs of smoke, select the Wacky Pencil tool, black, and medium width and draw the smoke.

5. The writing is done by using the Type Text found in the GOODIES menu. Select the tool and choose one of the small fonts from the bottom of the screen. Click in the puff of smoke and type in the words "I think I can."

6. To title the picture, choose Type Text from the GOODIES menu and a large font.

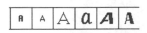

7. Click where you want the title. Hold down the shift key, press the quote mark key, and type in "I Think I Can" and another quote mark.

8. Save your picture by selecting Save from the FILE menu. Type in (I Think I Can:your initials) for the title and then click Save.

9. Print your picture.

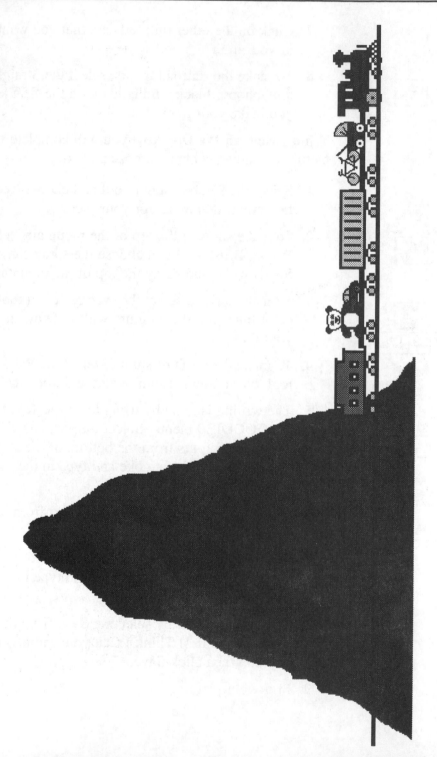

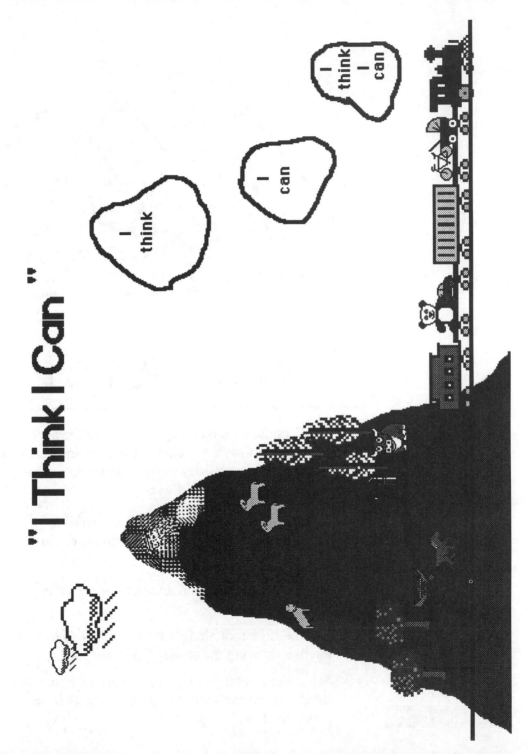

Building a Pyramid

InfoNet: Pyramids are buildings that house the ancient tombs of Egyptian royalty. They have a square base and four sloping, triangular sides meeting at the top. The Great Pyramids are found at Giza, Egypt.

This Project: In this project you will be building an Egyptian pyramid and showing the environment in which it was built.

1. Select the Line tool and smaller line width to make the basic triangle.

2. Use the Line tool along with the shift key to make the line showing the stones that were used.

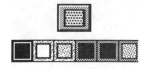

3. Select the Rectangle tool, the color black, the and filled box pattern from the menu at the bottom, to make the door.

4. Select the Rubber Stamp tool and choose the sphinx from the Companion assortment. There is also an Egyptian head and upper body that you can add to the picture. Use the Wacky Pencil to make the rest of the figure.

5. To turn the face in another direction, select Edit Stamp from the GOODIES menu in KP. If you are using KPS, select Edit Stamp from the TOOLBOX menu. Click on the top arrow to change the direction of your stamp. Click OK, and the stamp is changed.

6. Use the Paint Can tool to fill in the stones. You may want to choose various patterns and shades to make the stones look different.

7. Add other rubber stamps that are appropriate.

8. Use the Paint Can tool to add the sand.

9. Save and then print your project.

What Else Can We Do: Adding hieroglyphics, which are pictures or symbols representing words, to the picture gives it an even more authentic feel.

1. Use the Wacky Pencil tool to write your own hieroglyphics in the picture.

2. Use this picture as the cover of a report on ancient history.

3. This picture can be saved and used as a part of a slide show. If you want to add sound to your picture, you have 32 seconds to record. Select Record a Sound from the GOODIES menu.

4. Add more screens telling the purpose of the pyramids as a part of your presentation.

5. You could use this picture as the cover on a report about the current state of the pyramids.

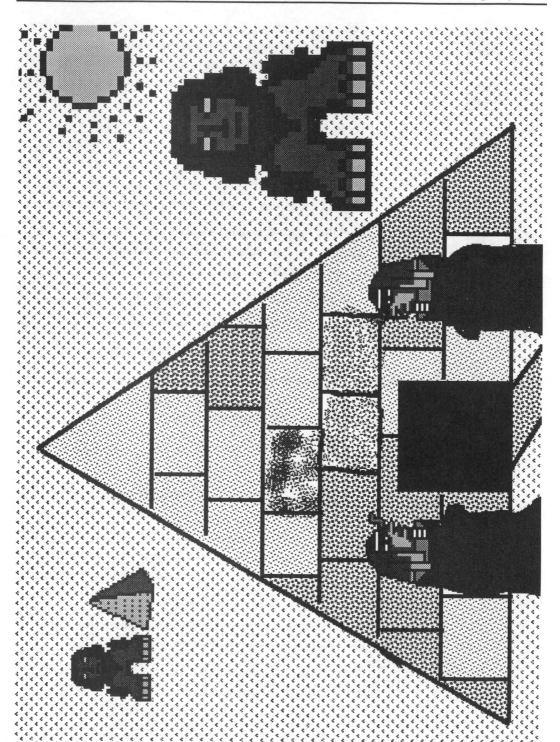

Make a Meal

InfoNet: The effect of healthy food choices on our daily diet has been the subject of much media coverage in the last few years. In planning food choices for the day, we need to take into consideration eating selections from certain food groups.

This Project: In this project you are going to choose foods that make a healthy breakfast, lunch, or dinner and put them on a plate. After completing this, you are going to construct a food pyramid that shows which foods are placed in each grouping.

1. What is your favorite meal of the day? Think about your favorite meal and which foods you know are healthy to eat at that meal. You need to choose a food from each of the following food groups: protein, breads and grains, dairy, fruits, and vegetables.

2. First make a plate for your food. To make the plate, select the Oval tool and the empty box pattern. Hold down the mouse button, click on the screen, and drag the mouse diagonally.

3. Now you need to choose the best foods for the meal.

4. Select the Rubber Stamp tool. Click on the arrow to the right to see more choices.

5. To find even more choices in KP, click on the SWITCHEROO menu and drag to Swap Stamps. Double-click on a stamp set you want to see. In KPS, go to the GOODIES menu and select Pick a Stamp Set. Double-click on a stamp set to choose your foods.

6. Click on a food to choose it and then click on the plate that you drew. Add all the foods that would be good for that meal.

What Else Can We Do: Adding two more plates to your picture will give you the chance to show all the good foods you should eat each day.)

1. Follow the directions on cards 1, 2, and 3 to make two more plates of food.
2. Label each part of the plate by its proper meal.
3. Select the Typewriter tool in KPS; in KP go to the GOODIES menu at the top of the screen and select Type Text. Click on one of the letters at the bottom of the screen. Click on the screen where you want your title and type it in.
4. Click on the screen over or under the plate and type Breakfast, Lunch, or Dinner, respectively.
5. You may title your picture "Three Good Meals."
6. To print your meal picture, go to the FILE menu and select print. Choose the size you want and click OK.
7. If you make the plate the size of the drawing screen and add the largest size of rubber stamps, when you print your picture it will be as large as a regular plate. Try pasting it on a paper plate.
8. Try printing the breakfast meal, the lunch meal, and the dinner meal pictures in small size. Cut the plates out and paste them on the front of a paper plate to show a whole day's food.

9. To make the food pyramid, use a clear screen and select the Line tool and draw a triangle.
10. Use the Line tool and the shift key to draw the lines that divide the triangle into sections.
11. Label each section to show fat, protein, and carbohydrates.

12. Select the Rubber Stamp tool and choose foods that fit into each food group.
13. Title your picture and then print it.

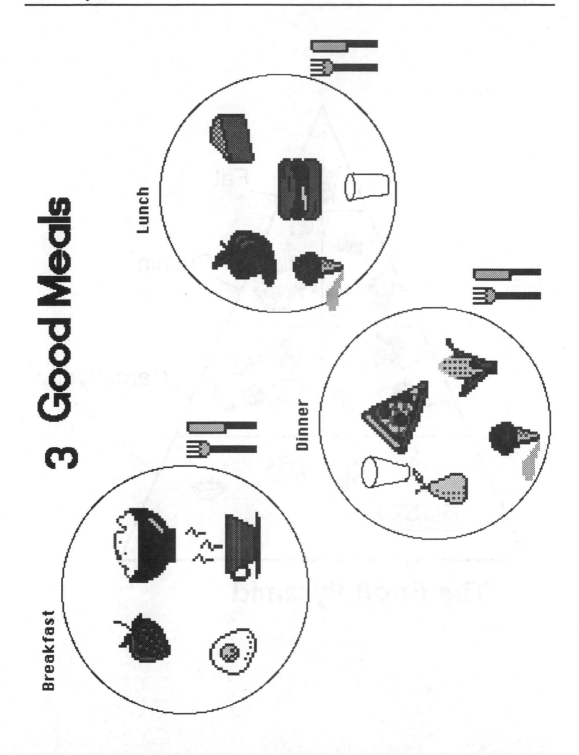

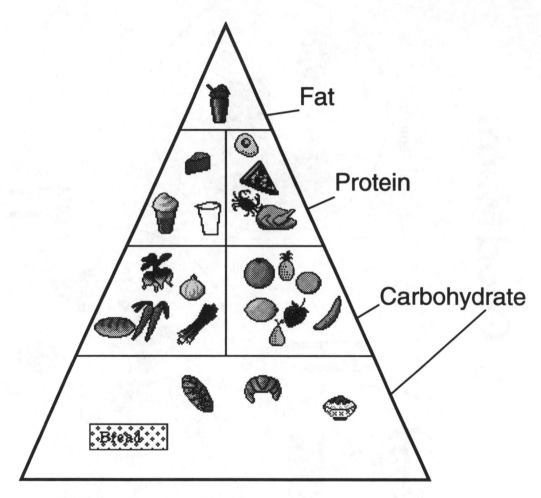

Fat

Protein

Carbohydrate

Bread

The Food Pyramid

A View of the Earth

InfoNet: The planet Earth is made up of layers which are the core, mantle, and crust. It is the fifth largest planet in the solar system and the third in distance from the sun.

This Project: You are going to draw the Earth as if it were cut in two and you are looking inside of it.

1. First, you will need to make the core of the earth. Select the Oval tool. Choose the empty box pattern at the bottom of the screen. Hold down the shift key and drag the mouse across the screen to make the outline of the inner core.

2. To make the mantle of the Earth, place the mouse about one-fourth inch (.625 cm) from the edge of the outer circle and pull diagonally to one-fourth inch (.625 cm) from the other side. Remember, you can always click on the Undo Guy to erase your last move.

3. Next make the crust of the Earth. Place the mouse about one-half inch (1.25 cm) from the outer circle and pull diagonally across the screen to make the crust.

4. Select the Paint Can tool. Choose a very lightly textured fill for the core. Click in the center of the core to fill.

5. Choose another lightly textured fill for the mantle and then fill it.

6. Choose a darker fill for the crust.

7. Select Type Text from the GOODIES menu and label the layers of the Earth.

What Else Can We Do: Now you can finish your picture by showing the area surrounding the Earth.

1. First draw the Earth's neighbor, the moon. Use the Oval tool, the color yellow, and the solid pattern option. Place the moon close to the earth.

2. To make the sun, select the Wacky Pencil tool, yellow and draw part of a circle in the upper-right hand corner.

3. Use the Paint Can tool and yellow to fill the sun.

4. Use Type Text from the GOODIES menu to label the sun and the moon.

5. Select the Wacky Brush tool and find the stars option to put stars in your picture.

6. To make the sky, select the Paint Can and then blue and click on the screen.

7. Use Type Text to title your picture.

8. Save and then print your project.

9. You may want to draw the planets in the solar system, using the tools that you used in making this project.

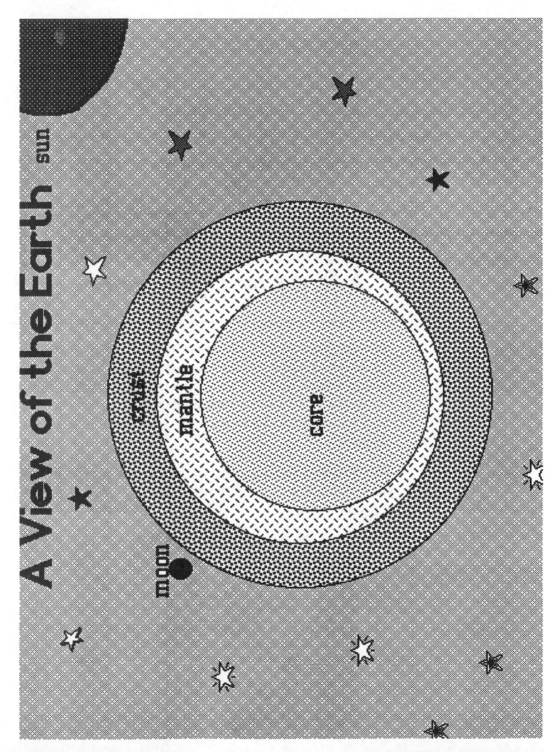

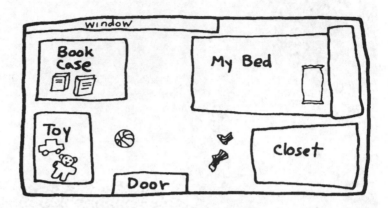

A Blueprint of My Room

InfoNet: Your bedroom is a part of the architecture of the whole house, but it is unique in that it is the place for your private special items. Often children don't have their own rooms but share a room with another family member. This takes careful planning to make the best possible use of space.

This Project: You are going to draw a bird's-eye view of your room. You then get to rearrange your room any way that you want.

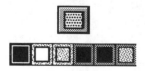

1. Select the Rectangle tool and the empty box option and then draw a large rectangle on the screen. This will serve as the outline of your room.

2. To show the location of the doors and windows, use the Eraser tool and small option to erase the sections of the outside outline of your room for the windows and doors.

3. Using the Rubber Stamp tool, select the items that belong in your room and place them where you want them. Remember that you can enlarge the stamps by using the shift key, the option key, or the shift and option keys together if you are on a Macintosh or use the control and shift keys on a PC.

4. Use the Rectangle tool, the empty box option, and the shift key to draw a legend for your room.

5. Label the doors with a D and the windows with a W. Now add the windows and doors to your legend.

What Else Can We Do: Now use the Moving Van tool to rearrange your room. Keep in mind the placement of windows and doors and the traffic pattern.

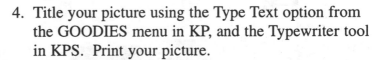

1. To move your furniture around, select the Moving Van tool and the magnet option.

2. Click near the object to be moved and move your mouse diagonally across the item. Put your mouse in the center of the box that you made and move it over to where you want to put your item.

3. If you want to keep the item in one place and put another one exactly like it in another place, hold down the option key while you are moving the mouse, and you will be making a copy of the original.

4. Title your picture using the Type Text option from the GOODIES menu in KP, and the Typewriter tool in KPS. Print your picture.

5. You may want to take a piece of construction paper to use as a base, print many types of furniture, cut out the pictures, and paste them onto the construction paper.

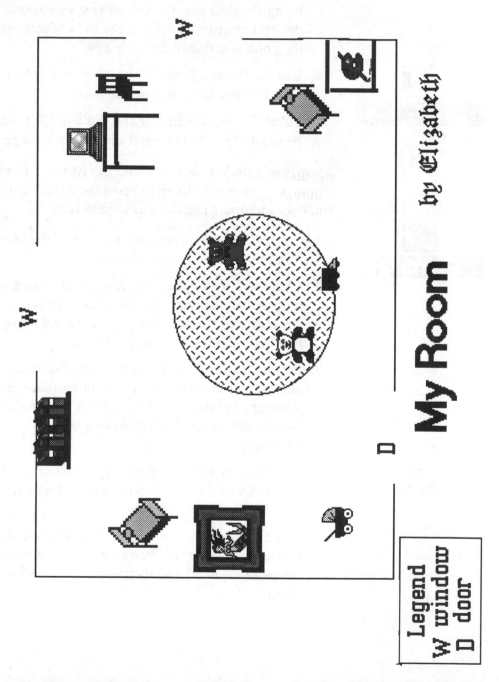

A Year in the Life of a Tree

InfoNet: There are two types of trees—evergreen and deciduous. The evergreen keep its leaves (needles) all year long, and the deciduous trees lose their leaves in the autumn.

This Project: You are going to follow the life of a deciduous tree through one full year, noting the changes in each season. You will be making a spring tree, summer tree, autumn tree, and winter tree.

1. Select the Wacky Brush option and click on the down arrow at the bottom of the screen to reach the level where you find a tree.

2. Click on the tree option and the color brown.

3. Move your cursor to the middle part of the screen. Hold down the option key and click.

4. Start by adding some elements to your picture that show it is spring. To make leaves for your spring tree, click on the arrow to go to the level where the bubbles are shown. Click on the bubbles option and the color green. Put some leaves on your tree.

5. Use the Wacky Pencil tool to draw roots for your tree. This is optional.

6. To add grass, select the Wacky Brush tool and locate the grass option. Click on the grass option and green. Move your mouse horizontally across the screen, holding the mouse button down.

7. Select the Rubber Stamp tool and look through the options to find birds, flowers, animals, and people to add to your picture.

8. In KP, select Type Text from the GOODIES menu. In KPS, select the Typewriter tool. Select a font from the bottom of the screen. Click on the screen and type in the word "Spring." Write a sentence about the effects of spring on a tree. Be sure to put your name on your picture.

9. Save and print your picture in the Itsy Bitsy size.

What Else Can We Do: Now you are going to make pictures that represent the other three seasons. After you print each of the four pictures, you will put them on a paper plate for display. Be sure to print each picture in Itsy Bitsy size.

1. To make your pictures into a display, use a paper plate as a base.

2. You can use the Electric Mixer tool and then choose the raindrop option on the far right to make snowflakes and/or rain.

3. You may want to print in large size to make a book.

4. To write a story about the tree passing through the year, choose a blank screen. Select Type Text from the GOODIES menu along with a large font for the title and then choose a smaller font for the story.

5. Save and print your story to accompany the pictures. (See page 207 for an example of a tree story.)

6. You can easily put your pictures into a slide show presentation. When you save your work put each screen into a folder that you have labeled "Seasons." Open the SlideShow screen and place each picture into a moving van. You can record a story about each picture by selecting the sound button. You have 32 seconds in which to record.

Example of a Fall Tree

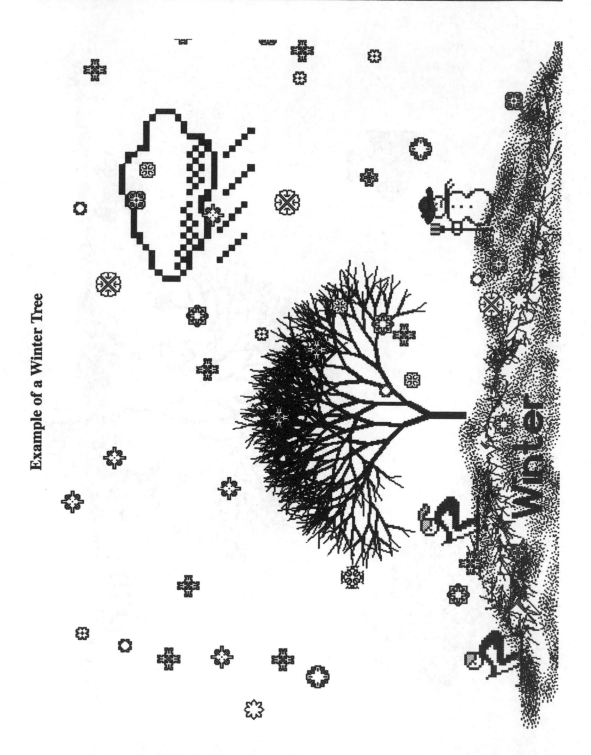

Example of a Winter Tree

Winter

Example of a Spring Tree

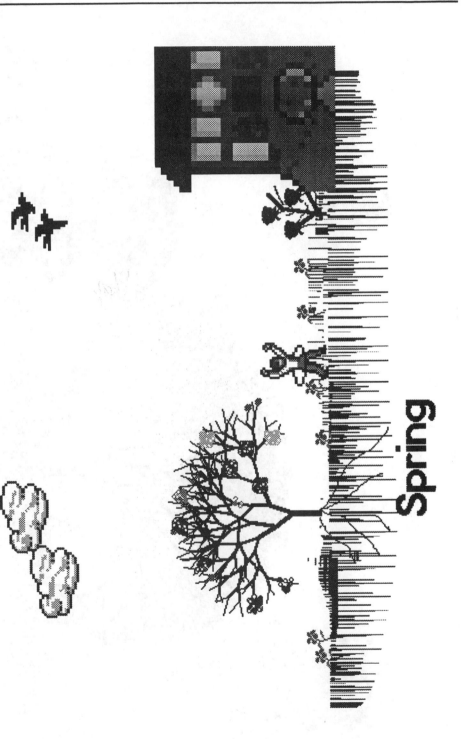

Example of a Summer Tree

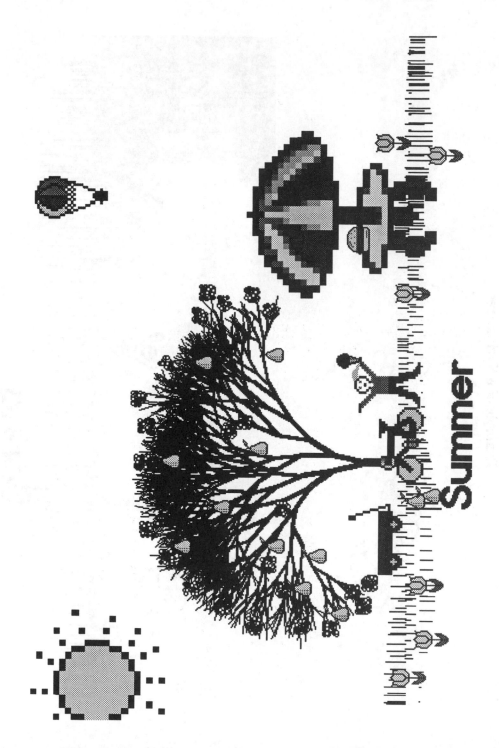

Summer

Example of a Tree Story

A Year in the Life of a Tree

My tree is happy in the Spring. The new leaves are coming. The grass is green all around her. My friends and I smell her blossoms.

In the summer we all play under her branches. Sometimes we eat near her. Her fruit tastes good to eat.

We jump in her leaves in the Fall. Even the Halloween ghost likes to swing in my tree.

In Winter the snow covers her branches and is on the ground. We ski near her.

Sample of Completed Project

Mapping a State

InfoNet: Each state has unique geographical and resource distinctions. Coastal states differ greatly from the landlocked states of the Midwest. Understanding the geography of a state helps in understanding the products produced by that state, as well as what recreational activities the inhabitants of the state enjoy.

This Project: In this project you will draw a state map and show its geographical regions.

1. Select the Wacky Pencil tool and a dark color. Draw the state you have selected. Remember, if you need straight lines, you can use the Line tool and hold down the shift key while drawing.

2. Title your picture. Select Type Text from the GOODIES menu.

3. Save your work at this point so that you will have a basic map on which to work in further projects. Save this, using the name of the state and the word outline (e.g., California Outline).

What Else Can We Do: Next, you will add the geographical regions and a legend to your map.

1. The above project can be the title page or the first slide of a slide show telling about your state.

2. You are now going to illustrate the regions of the state.

3. Use the Wacky Pencil tool and the thin or medium line width for your region outlines. Remember not to leave any openings or the fill will spill out.

4. Use a different color and pattern fill for each of the regions.

5. Select the Wacky Brush tool and use the spray can for the ocean, if you need one.

6. Select the Rectangle tool and hold down the shift key to make the correct number of boxes to represent the regions in your state map.

7. Use the Text tool to write in the name of each region.

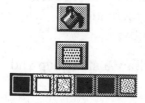

8. Select the Paint Can tool and the correct fill for each box.

9. To make the box around your legend, select the Rectangle tool and the empty box option.

10. Select Save As from the FILE menu.

11. Title your project, using the name of the state and the word regions (e.g., California Regions).

12. You are now going to add the state resources to your map.

13. Open your state regions map.

14. Select the Rubber Stamp option and choose the appropriate stamps to match the natural resources to the regions you want to illustrate. Remember to select Swap Stamps in the SWITCHEROO menu of KP, or Pick a Stamp Set in the GOODIES menu of KPS to change stamp groups.

15. Make a legend, using the Rectangle tool with empty box option, stamps, and the Text tool.

16. Select Save As from the FILE menu and title this with the state name and the word resources (e.g., California Resources).

17. You may want to make another map illustrating the products and industries of your state.

18. Arrange these screens into a slide show as an addition to a state report. You could also use the print outs as illustrations in your state report.

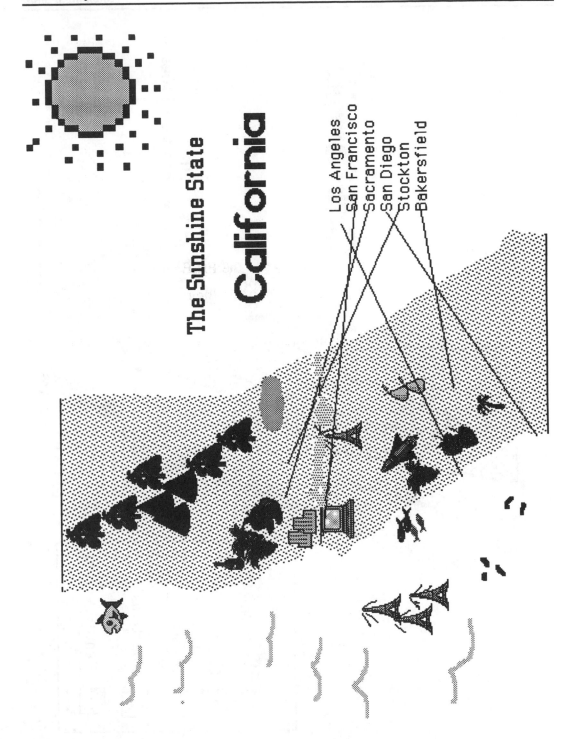

The Sunshine State

California

Los Angeles
San Francisco
Sacramento
San Diego
Stockton
Bakersfield

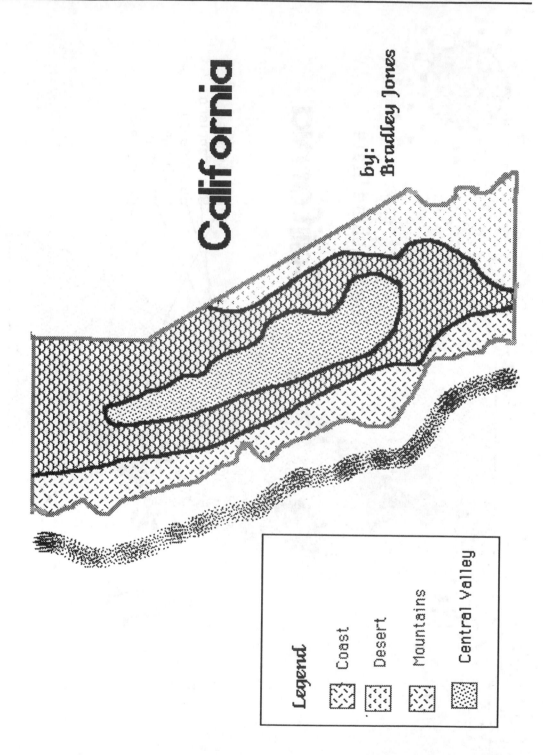

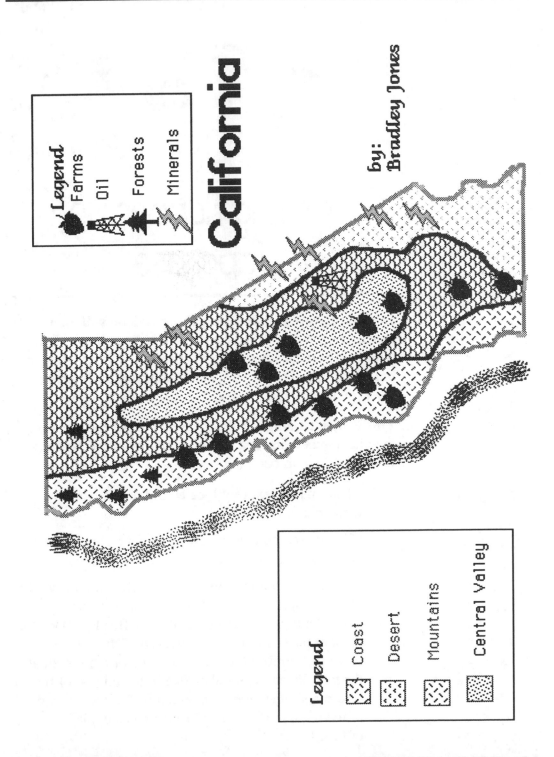

Writing Numbers in Japanese

InfoNet: Everyday Japanese writing is done with pen or pencil. Japanese character writing is called shodo. It is written in vertical lines from right to left, and it is done in brush and ink. There is a special order that each stroke must follow.

This Project: Using the Wacky Pencil tool, you are going to write numbers in Japanese and then write the Japanese words for the numbers.

1. Click on the Text tool located in the left-hand menu bar.

2. Click on the number arrow at the far right side and go to the level where the numbers are located.

3. Click on the number one and then click on the screen at the top left. The number one is now at the top. Place the two in the middle of the left side. Place the number three almost at the bottom of the screen. Place the number four at the middle of the screen at the top. Place the number five in the middle of the screen and place the number six at the bottom middle of the screen. (See page 216 for an example of this.)

4. Select the Wacky Pencil tool and the color black and then select the second line width from the left.

5. Use the sample page as a guide to draw in the number symbols one through six. **Note:** If you make a mistake, undo it with the Undo Guy or use the Eraser tool. (See page 216 for a sample of this.)

6. Select the Rubber Stamp tool. Choose the correct number of stamps to illustrate each number. Put the rubber stamps next to the Japanese numbers. (See page 217 for an example of this.)

7. To save your work, select Save from the FILE menu. Title this project "Japanese Numbers." To print your numbers, select Print from the FILE menu.

What Else Can We Do: Now you are going to add the Japanese words for each number.

1. In KP, select Type Text from the GOODIES menu. In KPS, select the Typewriter tool. Choose a font that you like from the bottom of the screen.

2. Click the mouse right under the numeral. Then type in the Japanese number word. (See page 218 for an example of this.)

1	ichi	6	roku
2	ni	7	shichi
3	san	8	hachi
4	shi	9	ku
5	go	10	ju

3. Now try writing the number word in another language under the Japanese.

Spanish:		**French:**	
uno	seis	un	six
dos	siete	deux	sept
tres	ocho	trois	huit
cuatro	nueve	quatre	neuf
cinco	diez	cinq	dix

4. Save and print your number page.

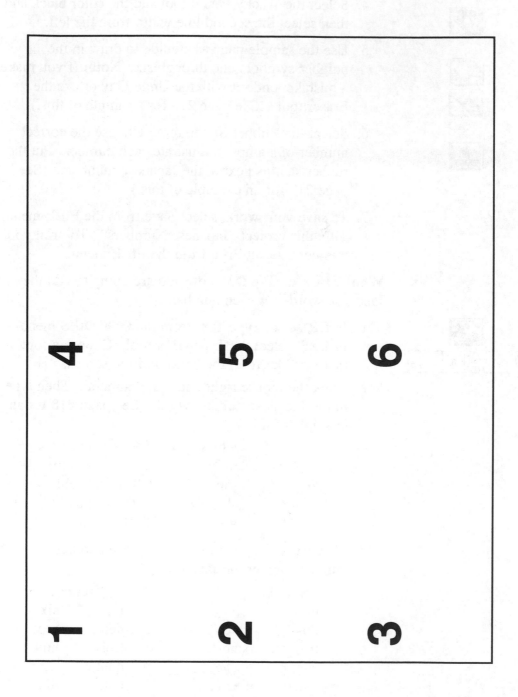

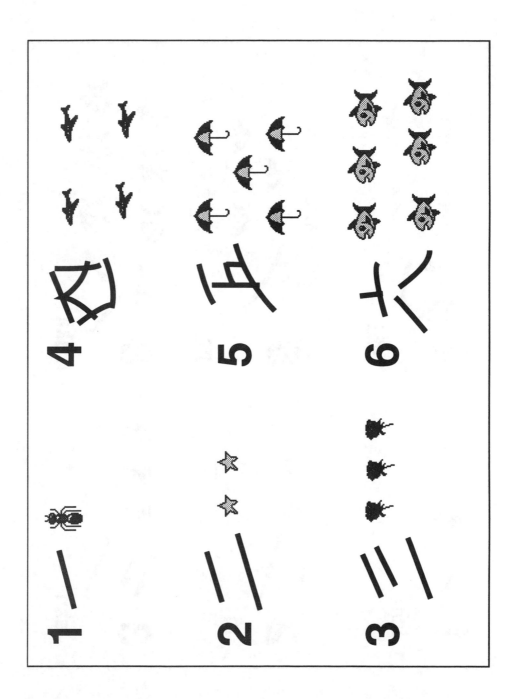

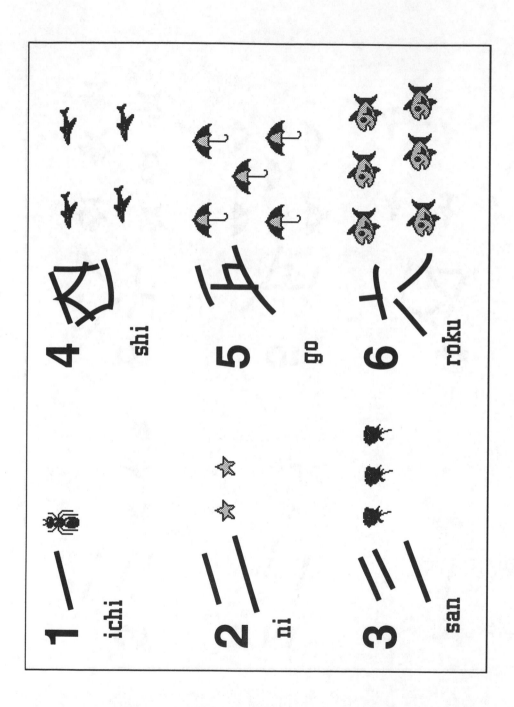

Uncle Sam Clothespin Puppet for the Fourth of July

InfoNet: The figure of Uncle Sam represents the people and the government of the United States of America. He is usually shown as a tall, thin man with whiskers on his chin and dressed in a red, white, and blue costume of a long coat, striped pants, and a tall hat with a band of stars.

This Project: In this project you are going to draw a picture of Uncle Sam, print it, and then cut it out and put it on a clothespin to make an Uncle Sam clothespin puppet.

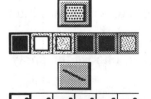

1. To draw the body, select the Rectangle tool and empty box pattern and then draw a long rectangle in the middle of the screen.

2. To make the waist and pants, choose the Line tool and a small line width.

3. Hold down the shift key and draw a line across the rectangle for the waist.

4. Hold down the shift key and draw a vertical line from the waist down to make the pants.

5. To make the arms you will need to use the Oval and Rectangle tools.

6. Select the Oval tool and the empty box pattern and then draw an oval about one inch (2.5 cm) from the body to make the hand.

7. Select the Rectangle tool and empty box pattern and then make a rectangle that connects the body to the hand.

8. Now make the head, using the Oval tool and holding down the shift key as you draw.

9. Use the Oval tool to draw the feet.

10. Select the Line tool and filled box pattern and then draw a tall, thin rectangle for the hat.

11. Color in the hat by choosing the Paint Can, any color, and clicking in the center of the hat outline.

12. Choose the Line tool, hold down the shift key, and then draw the hat's brim.

What Else Can We Do: Now it is time to dress Uncle Sam in his costume.

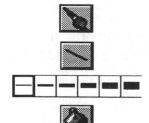

1. Select the Wacky Brush tool and draw in the bottom of his coat.

2. Choose the Line tool and thin line width to draw the strips on his pants.

3. Select the Paint Can tool and the red, white, and blue colors to fill in his clothes.

4. To make the beard and tufts of hair, choose the spray can option in Wacky Brush.

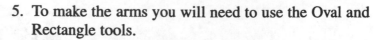

5. Select the Rubber Stamp tool and find a star stamp to put on Uncle Sam's hat.

6. Save and print your version of Uncle Sam. Cut out your picture and glue it to a clothespin.

A Fearsome Dragon Diorama

InfoNet: Dragons, or mythical monsters, have played an important part in storytelling throughout the ages. Sometimes they were depicted as having wings and claws and breathing out fire and smoke.

This Project: In this project you are going to make an imaginative fearsome dragon diorama to use in storytelling.

1. To make the body, select the Oval tool and click and drag the oval across the screen.

2. Select the Wacky Pencil tool and draw the spines on the dragon's back.

3. Draw the head, using the Wacky Pencil tool.

4. Make the eyes and nostrils, using the Oval tool while holding down the shift key.

5. Finish your drawing, using the Wacky Pencil tool and any other tools that you think will help you create your picture.

6. Select the Paint Can to fill any areas that need color.

What Else Can We Do: Now you will take your dragon and put it into a diorama.

1. Print your dragon in the small size. Paste the dragon onto stiff paper such as cardboard or tagboard. (**Note:** Your teacher should be able to provide the heavy paper for you.)

2. Cut out the dragon.

3. Now you will need to make the background for the diorama.

4. On a blank screen, choose and place the rubber stamps that you need for the background. You may want to use the castle stamped in the largest size. Hold down the shift and option keys while you stamp.

5. Print the background in the medium size.

6. Paste the background on the back of the shoe box and place the dragon in front. You could bend some of the leg back and paste it down.

Dragon Diorama

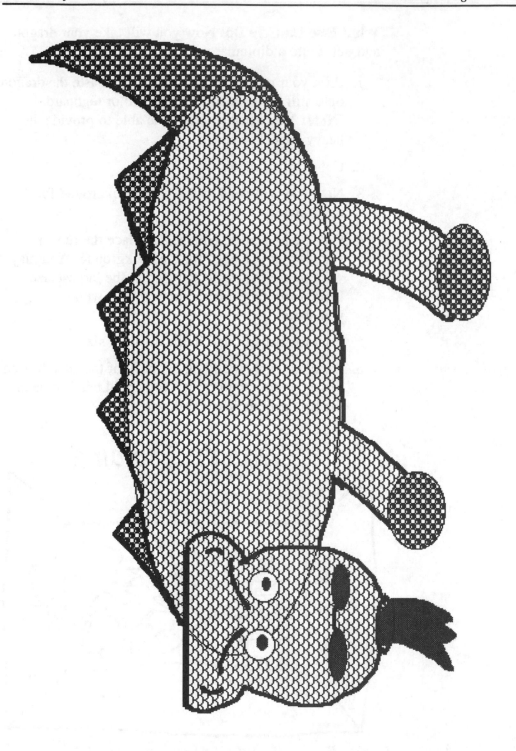

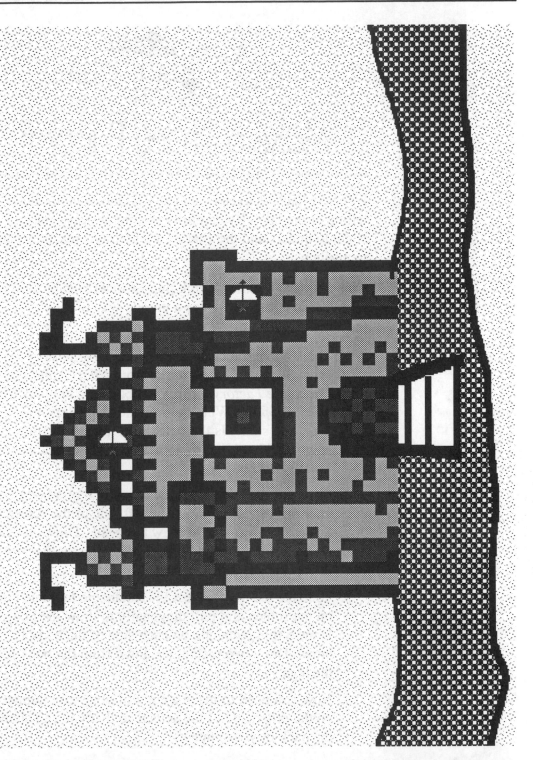

Make a Story Puppet

InfoNet: Each character in a story is important to the telling of the tale. By carefully reading a story, you can begin to understand the character's feelings, reactions, and motivation.

This Project: Making a stick puppet that resembles a character in a story provides a unique way of retelling the story.

1. Think about the character in your favorite story. For example, it could be Charlie from *Charlie and the Chocolate Factory*, or it could be Mary Poppins from *Mary Poppins*. What color is the characters hair, eyes, and skin? Is the hair short, long, or medium length? What kind of clothes does the character usually wear?

2. First, you will need to draw an outline of a body for your puppet. Draw it on the left side of the screen. Select the Oval tool to draw the head. Draw an oval or circle for the head. To draw a circle, hold down the option key while drawing.

3. To make the body, select the Rectangle tool and click on the screen and pull diagonally to draw the body. Draw a thin rectangle on each side of the body for arms. Draw two rectangles down from the body for the legs.

4. Now you need to make a copy of your base puppet on the other side of the screen so that you can show the back of your puppet.

5. Select the Moving Van tool and click on the magnet in the option menu.

6. Move your mouse to the upper left-hand corner of the screen and pull diagonally until your body is inside of the box.

7. Now you are going to move the body puppet to the other side of the screen while leaving the original one in the left part of the screen.

8. Hold the mouse button down; the magnet shows you where the mouse is. Hold the option key down. Holding the option key down keeps the original puppet where you drew it.

9. Move the mouse to the right side of the screen and the body comes with it. (See page 228 for an example of this.)

What Else Can We Do: Now it is time to add the clothes to the puppet.

1. Select the Wacky Pencil tool to draw the clothes.

2. Draw the same outline of the clothes on the puppet on the right side of the screen.

3. Use the Paint Can tool to fill in the clothes.

4. Use the Rubber Stamp tool to create patterns and designs on the clothes.

5. To fill in the skin color, use the Paint Can tool and choose a color close to your skin color.

6. A fun way to draw hair is using the Wacky Brush tool and the hay option. Select the color for your hair. Hold down the option key as you draw to make the hair thicker.

7. Be sure that the back of your puppet matches the front.

8. Print the puppet page.

9. Cut out the two puppets and glue them onto a craft stick.

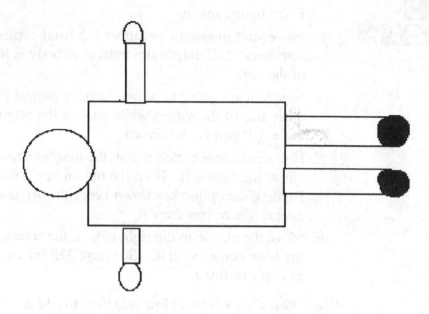

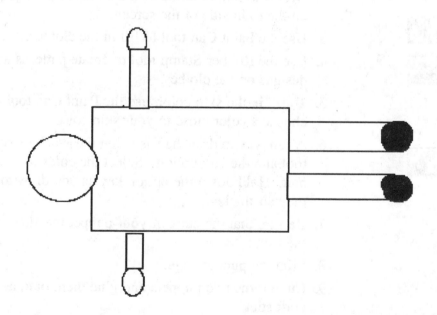

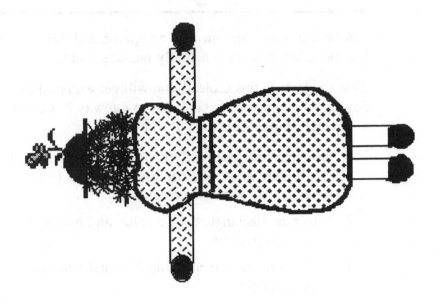

Design a Car

InfoNet: It is first designed by computer, and then a model is created before a car is actually manufactured.

This Project: In this project, you will get a chance to design your own vehicle similarly to the way it is done at the manufacturers—carved out of a block.

1. Use your imagination to mentally design a special car; be sure to include some of the basics (e.g., chassis, tires, windows, etc.).

2. Select the Rectangle tool, a color, and one of the more solid patterns.

3. Click on the screen and drag diagonally to make a large rectangle.

4. Select the Eraser tool and one of the four erasers on the left-hand side of the screen. It is probably easier to use the circle eraser. Select white and click on the screen.

5. Hold down the mouse button as you use the eraser to carve your car.

6. Use the Oval tool to make the tires and the headlights. Fill with color.

7. Click on the Rubber Stamp tool.

8. To put some people in your vehicle, go to the SWITCHEROO menu in KP and select Swap Stamps. In KPS select Pick a Stamp Set from the GOODIES menu.

9. Choose some people and place them in your vehicle. Use rubber stamps or drawing tools to complete your picture.

10. Save and print.

How Does It Taste?

InfoNet: Different parts of the tongue give taste various flavors. The tongue tastes for sweet, sour, salt, and bitter in different areas.

This Project: Drawing the tongue and the different taste areas helps you to remember the tongue's job.

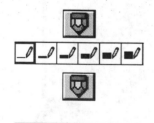

1. Select the Wacky Pencil tool and the medium line thickness to draw an outline of the tongue.

2. Select the Wacky Pencil tool and draw lines showing the different tasting parts of the tongue.

3. Select Type Text from the GOODIES menu and then select a font from the bottom of the screen.

4. Type in the type of taste for each area of the tongue.

What Else Can We Do: You can add pictures that illustrate the various taste areas of the tongue.

1. Select the Rubber Stamp tool and look for pictures that show the various tastes of the tongue.

2. Use the arrow on the far right to go through the eight levels of stamps to choose pictures to go with the taste areas of the tongue.

3. To find more choices, in KP select Swap Stamps from the SWITCHEROO menu. In KPS, select Pick a Stamp Set from the GOODIES menu. Select a group and click OK and go through them to see if there are any pictures you can use for the areas of the tongue.

4. If you cannot find any rubber stamps for the tongue, use the Wacky Pencil tool to draw some of your own pictures.

5. Use the Oval tool and yellow to draw a lemon to illustrate sour. Use the Oval tool and green to draw a sour pickle.

6. Click on the Paint Can tool, choose pink, select an open pattern from the option menu, and click on the tongue to fill. If there are any openings in your drawing, the paint will spill onto the entire screen. If needed, use the Wacky Pencil tool to close any openings.

7. Save and then print your project.

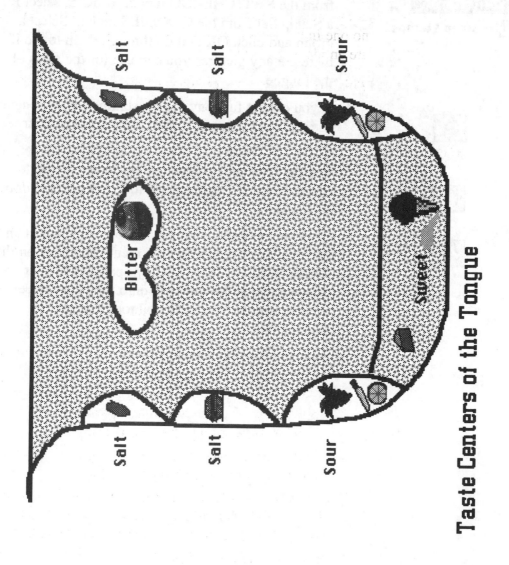

Taste Centers of the Tongue

A Personal Totem

InfoNet: All people have something special about them that makes them unique and different from others. This uniqueness makes us individuals. Remember that there is no one in the world exactly like you physically unless you are an identical twin.

This Project: You are going to create your own totem which will show the things that make you unique.

1. Select the Rubber Stamp tool and look through the stamps until you find someone who looks somewhat like you.

2. Click on the stamp that looks most like you. Now you can change the stamp to look even more like you. Select Edit Stamp from the GOODIES menu. This brings your stamp in large format so you can edit it.

3. Click on any color, hold the mouse button down, and move the mouse over the color you want to change.

4. When you are finished, click OK, and the picture changes in the stamp options. Hold down the option key and click your picture stamp at the top of the screen.

5. Now choose other stamps that represent your uniqueness and stamp them on the screen.

6. To write about each of your unique qualities, select Type Text from the GOODIES menu.

7. Choose a small font from the bottom of the screen, click next to each picture, and write about where it fits in your life. (See page 236 for an example.)

8. Title your picture and print it.

*See page 237 for an example cover for a biography or an autobiography.

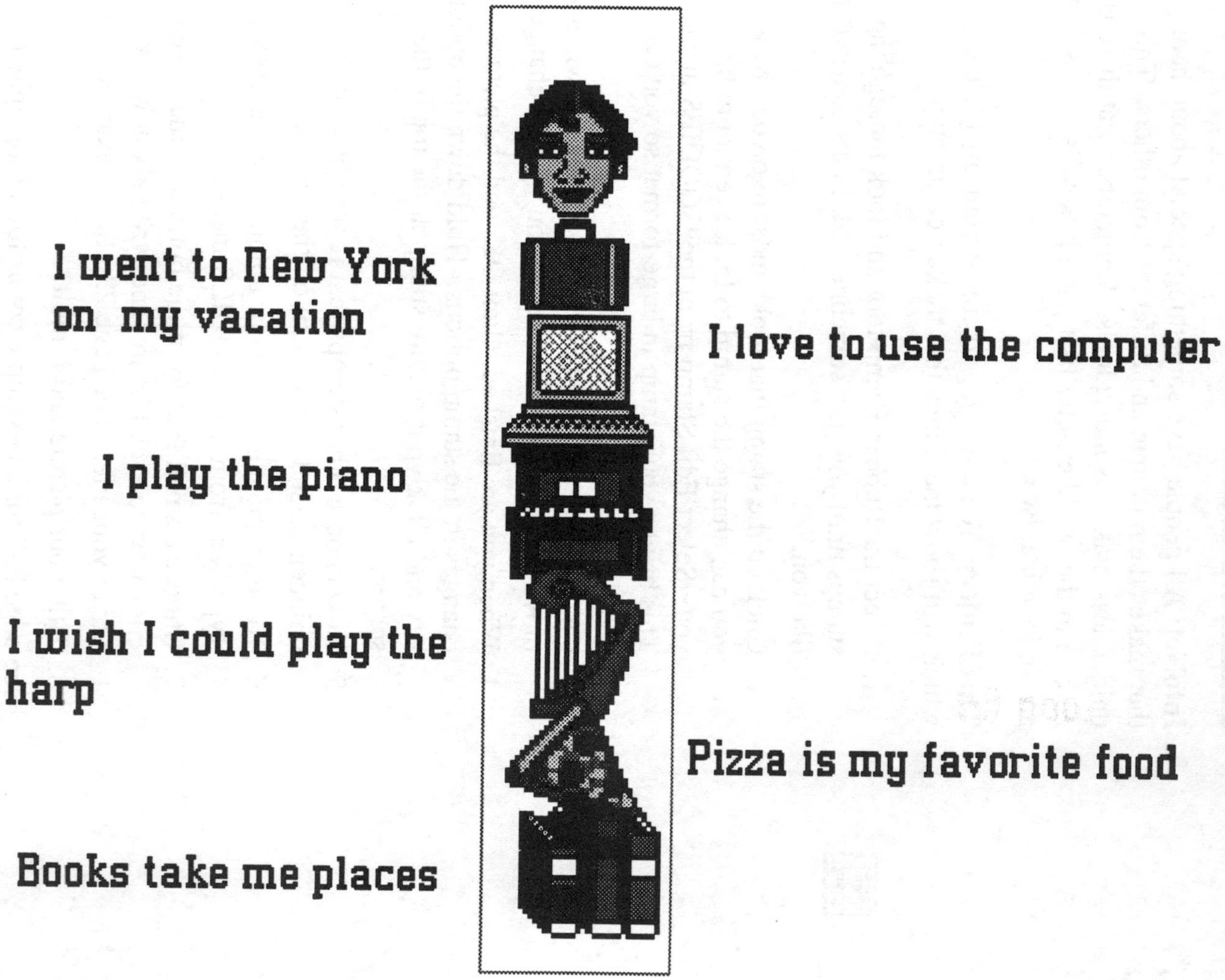

I love to use the computer

Pizza is my favorite food

I went to New York on my vacation

I play the piano

I wish I could play the harp

Books take me places

Paul was wood cutter

He wore big cowboy boots

He lived in the frontier days

He carried a weapon

His horse was huge

His blue ox was called Babe

Paul Bunyon - The Legend

Imitate Great Art

InfoNet: Most artists have a unique style of creating their work. Some, like Picasso, have several different styles. One of Picasso's styles is called cubism, where he made his paintings in a combination of geometric shapes. Seurat made his paintings using a process called pointillism in which the painting is made from hundreds of dots. Mondrian used rectangles to form his paintings.

This Project: This is your chance to paint in the style of one of the great artists of the world. You first need to see a copy of a painting done by one of these artists in order to try to copy the style. For this example you will draw in the manner of van Gogh, who used light colors in his art to illustrate the light captured in nature.

1. Select the Wacky Brush tool and the fractal tree option.

2. Choose brown and make a series of trees.

3. Choose yellow and make some fractal trees over the brown ones.

4. Select the Wacky Brush tool grass option and green.

5. Repeat the grass, using yellow.

6. Title your picture, using Type Text from the GOODIES menu. Type "In the Manner of van Gogh." (See page 240 for an example of this.)

7. Print your picture.

What Else Can We Do: Try drawing in another artist's style, this time similarly to Mondrian, who uses geometrics as a base for his work.

1. To make the basic sections of the art work, select the Rectangle tool and the empty box option.

2. Click at the edge of the screen and pull diagonally for the first shape. Continue making geometric shapes, making sure that each one touches another.

3. Select the Paint Can tool and the filled box option.

4. Fill each section, leaving some in white.

5. To make the dark lines between shapes, select the Line tool, medium width, and black.

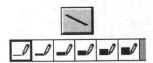

6. Hold down the shift key and trace the outlines of the shapes.

7. Use Type Text to title the picture "In the Manner of Mondrian." (See page 241 for an example of this.)

8. Print your picture.

9. To make a picture in the manner of Ellsworth Kelly, select the Wacky Pencil tool, medium line width, and black.

10. Draw a rectangle shape with rounded corners.

11. Fill, using the Paint Can tool, orange, and the filled box option.

12. Fill the rest of the drawing in green.

13. Title the picture, using Type Text "In the Manner of Ellsworth Kelly." (See page 242 for an example.)

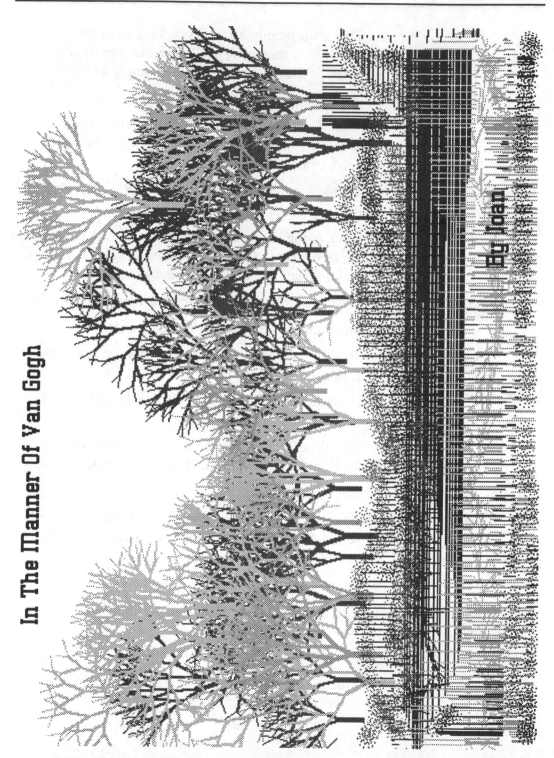

In The Manner Of Van Gogh

By Joan

In The Manner Of Ellsworth Kelly

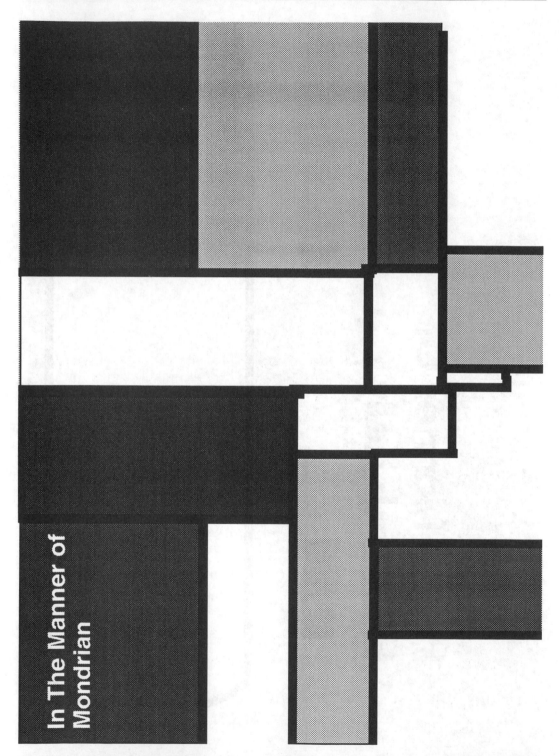

In The Manner of Mondrian

Personal Time Line

InfoNet: Time lines are visual representations of data. Working with data occurs in stages: collecting the data, entering the data onto the time line, and analyzing the data. Time lines can be constructed regarding any series of events from daily schedules to steps occurring in the production of a product.

This Project: You are going to construct a time line of your life and use graphics to illustrate the important events.

1. Decide which events you want to include on your time line. Note the date and the event. How many events will fit on the screen?

2. To draw the actual time line base, select the Line tool and use the shift key as you draw a line across the bottom part of the screen. Make straight vertical lines for each event you want to feature.

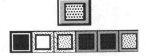

3. At the top of each vertical line use the Rectangle tool and empty box pattern to make a box in which to write the actual event.

4. In KP, select Type Text from the GOODIES menu. If you are using KPS, select the Typewriter tool and then choose a small font to write the event in each box.

5. Write the date of each event at the bottom of the vertical line.

6. Select the Rubber Stamp tool and browse through the stamps to find and place pictures that illustrate each of your events. You may need to draw matching pictures.

7. Print your project.

My Personal Time Line by Louise Jones

I was born in 1988	I first talked	I went to school	I was elected President of the 3rd grade	I went to Disneyland in June
1988	1990	1993	1996	1997

Hanukkah Dreidle

InfoNet: The dreidle used today is like the one used in Germany many years ago. On the dreidle are the Hebrew letters Nun, Gimmel, Hay, and Shin. They represent in Hebrew the message, "A great miracle happened there." They come in many sizes, shapes, and colors.

This Project: Making a four sided Hanukkah dreidle is fun to do using the Straight Line tool and the Wacky Pencil.

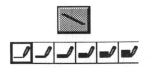

1. Select the Straight Line tool and medium width line. Hold down the shift key and pull your mouse across the screen near the top.

2. Draw a line down the middle of the screen.

3. Now divide each section in half. Make a line at each end.

4. Draw straight lines with the Straight Line tool, holding down the shift key. Make four points, one for each side of the dreidle.

5. Now you need to write the four Hebrew letters that are on the dreidle. Write one on each section of your dreidle.

שכגה

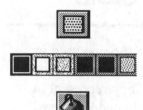

6. Use the Rectangle tool, solid pattern to make the handles on the dreidle. Click near the top of the dreidle and drag diagonally until you have a handle. You need to make one for each section.

7. Use the Paint Can to fill in the dreidle sections.

8. Print your dreidle.

What Else Can We Do: Now you can put your dreidle together.

1. Cut out your dreidle along the dark lines on the outside.

2. Fold on the three lines.

3. Tape the open ends together. Your dreidle is complete.

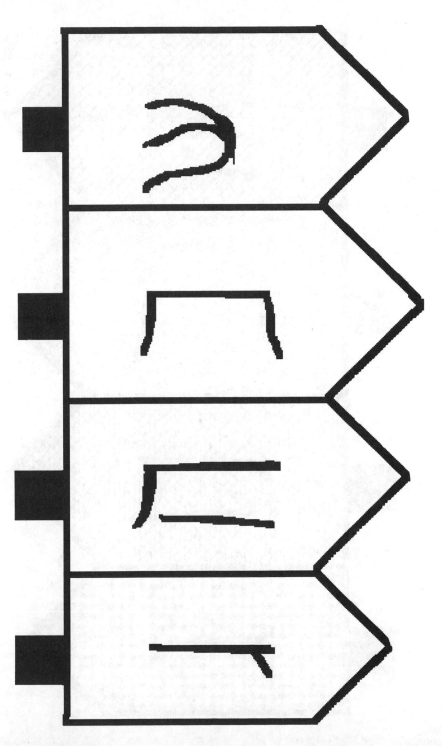

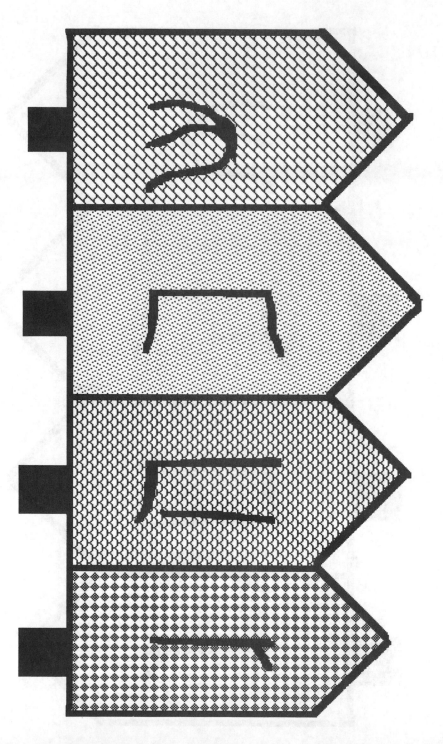

Valentine Pop-Up Card

InfoNet: The original Valentine cards were funny, not at all romantic and generally were sent by men who did not sign their names. Today Valentine cards and gifts are sent to friends and loved ones by both men and women.

This Project: In this project you are going to make a special Valentine's Day card on the computer to give to someone special.

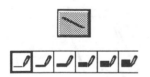

1. First you will divide the drawing screen in half. Select the Straight Line tool and medium line thickness. Start your line at the top of the screen, in the center by holding down the shift key and drawing your line to the bottom of the screen.

2. Now that you have divided your card into two smaller rectangles, you are going to write a message at the bottom of the rectangle on the left side. This will eventually become the outside of the card. Select Type Text from the GOODIES menu. Click on the bottom left side of the left rectangle and type in your message.

3. To make the inside of the card, select the Rubber Stamp tool and then the red heart. Hold down the shift and option keys as you stamp your heart in the middle of the right rectangle.

4. To add a message to the inside of the card, select Type Text from the GOODIES menu. Click the mouse where you want your message and type it in. (See page 252 for a sample Valentine's Day card before it is put together.)

What Else Can We Do: Just follow the directions carefully to make the card.

1. Print your card.

2. Fold your card along the center line and then make a cut along your fold, until you have cut it in half and now have two pieces of paper. One is going to be the cover of your card and the other is going to be the inside of your card.

3. Placing both pieces of paper together, fold your card in half from top to bottom, so that your picture is inside.

4. Make one cut on each side of your picture about 2"
   (5 cm) long.

5. Fold the card again, but this time push the cut
   piece out.

6. Glue the two pieces of paper together back-to-back,
   making sure not to glue the pop-up part.

7. See page 253 for the completed Valentine's Day card.

Sample Valentine's Day Card

Completed Valentine's Day Pop-Up Card

Thematic Paper Chain

InfoNet: When you compare and contrast the habitats, people, geography, foods, and recreation of various countries, you find a common thread among them.

This Project: You will be creating a paper chain depicting different parts of the countries or places that you choose. On each of the rectangles that you make you will put rubber stamps that depict a particular country. After you print, you can cut apart the rectangles and make them into a paper chain.

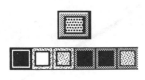

1. Select the Rectangle tool from the menu and the empty box pattern from the options menu.

2. Starting at the upper left-hand corner click and drag diagonally to make a long and thin rectangle. To duplicate more of these rectangles on the page, select the Moving Van tool and the magnet option. Encircle the rectangle within the flashing lines.

3. Put the magnet cursor inside the rectangle and hold down the option key. Click and move the rectangle slightly to the left. Remember to hold down the option key or loose the first rectangle.

4. Repeat this process until you have five rectangles on the page. (See page 256 for an example of this.)

5. It is now time to put rubber stamps on the rectangles. Select the Rubber Stamp tool and review the stamp options. Place four rubber stamps on each rectangle and then write the name of the country or area that you are depicting at the bottom using the Typewriter tool or Type Text from the GOODIES menu.

6. After your strips are finished print them out.

7. Using a scissors cut each strip and fasten the ends of the first one together with glue or a staple. Put the next strip through the first circle and fasten. Continue until all the strips are used. You now have a paper chain that you may wish to enlarge upon.

What Else Can We Do: Now that you have completed one paper chain. You can make a paper chain on almost any topic or theme.

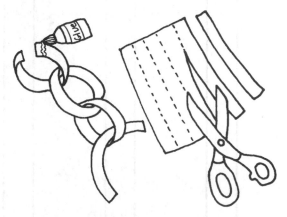

1. Make a paper chain that tells about you, your favorite foods, your friends, activities you like to participate in, and your family.

2. Your teacher can use the chains to make a giant chain that loops across the bulletin board or across the front of the room.

3. Make a paper chain to accompany a science report on which you can group animals or habitats.

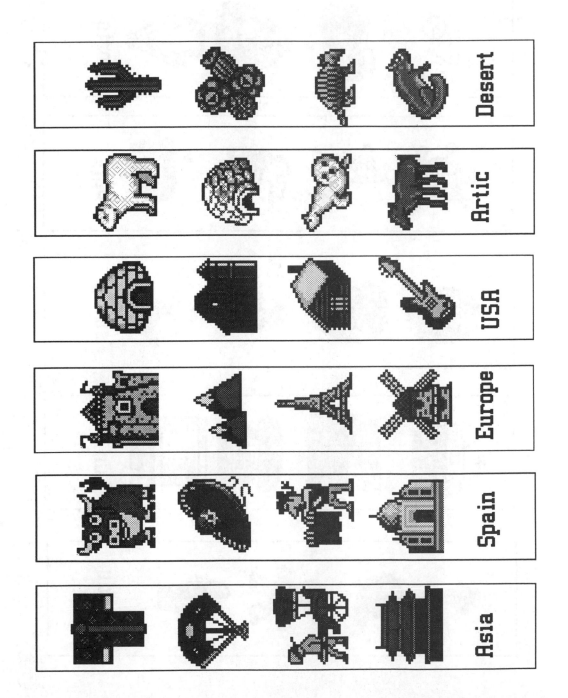

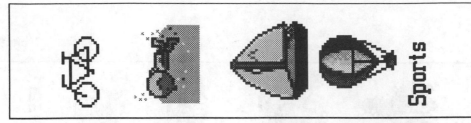

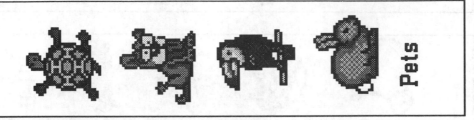

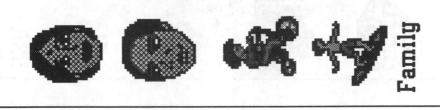

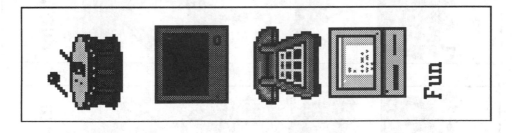

Rockets Red Glare

InfoNet: Rockets are often times propelled by a gas rocket fuel. When ignited this fuel gives the rocket the energy and momentum needed for it to launch into the sky and enables people to see its trail with the naked eye.

This Project: You are going to modify an existing rubber stamp as part of a picture showing the burning of the rocket fuel.

1. Select the rocket from the Rubber Stamps tool. Then select the Edit Stamp from the GOODIES menu. (See page 261 for example of the Edit Stamp.)

2. Click on the white in the color palette. To erase the black around the edges of the rocket, click on each black pixel. When you are finished, click OK.

3. Notice that the rubber stamp at the bottom of the screen has no black outline. Click on that stamp, hold down the option and shift keys as you stamp the rocket on the screen.

4. Use the Wacky Pencil tool to draw part of the earth in the lower right-hand corner of the screen. You may want to draw in part of the ocean on your picture of the earth.

5. Now it is time to add the burning rocket fuel to the picture. Select the Wacky Brush tool, the spray can option, and the color red to make fuel trail.

6. Add the planets that are next to earth by using the Wacky Pencil tool and fills or the Oval tool and fills.

7. To add some stars, you can use the stars option in the Wacky Brush tool.

8. To complete your picture, use the Paint Can tool and an appropriate color to make the sky.

What Else Can We Do: Your rocket picture can be a great start to a slide show on rockets, a report on rockets, or you can even use it as the background on a story for traveling into space.

1. Use the rocket picture as part of a slide show on rockets. Save the picture and import it into one of the moving vans for the slide show. In planning your show be sure to use the Kid Pix Storyboard on page 296.

2. Add text to your picture using the Typewriter tool or select Type Text from the GOODIES menu and use it as the cover for a science report.

3. Write a story about how it feels to be in a space capsule as you leave the earth's atmosphere, using your picture as the background.

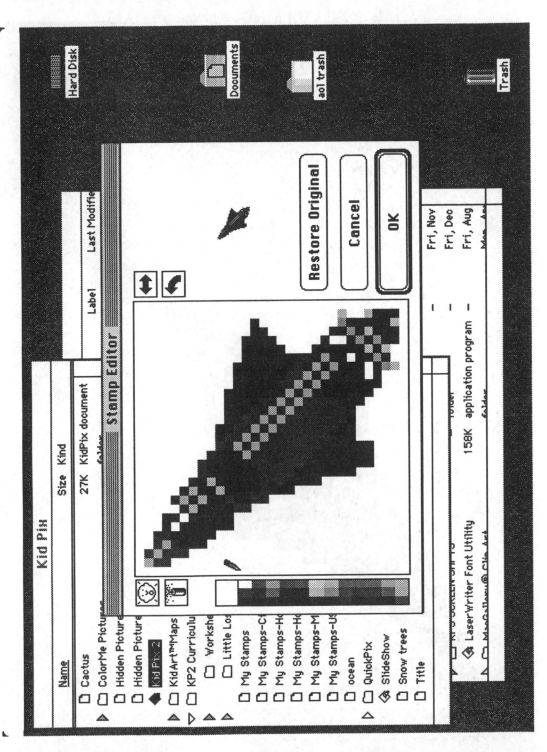

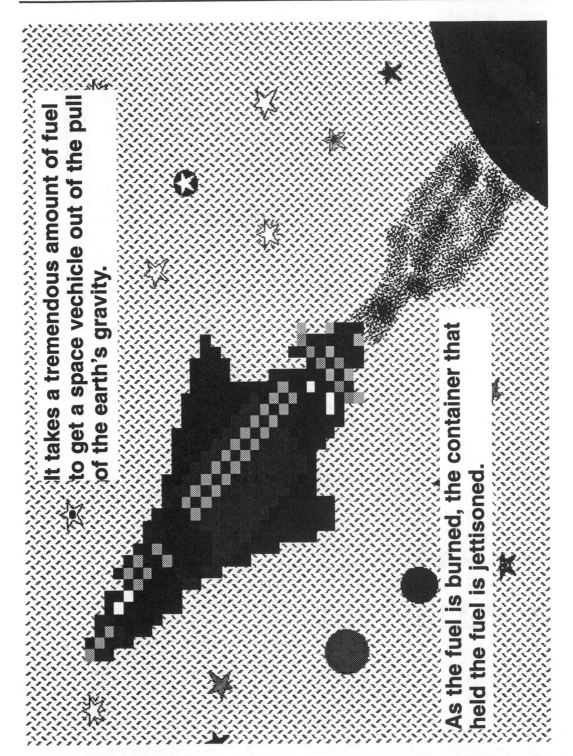

It takes a tremendous amount of fuel to get a space vechicle out of the pull of the earth's gravity.

As the fuel is burned, the container that held the fuel is jettisoned.

My Weekly Schedule

InfoNet: When you see all the activities that you do in one week, you will be amazed. By making a pictorial weekly schedule you may find that you can reschedule some of your activities to make better use of your time. This is called "Time Management" in the professional working world.

This Project: You will be making a pictorial schedule of all of your weekly activities and then print them out.

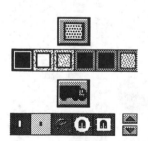

1. Select the Rectangle tool and the empty box option to make the outlines of your schedule. Make a vertical rectangle at the top of your screen. Select the Moving Van tool and the magnet option. Encircle the rectangle within the moving van lines. Hold down the mouse button and the option key, while you move the rectangle to the bottom part of the screen.

2. Select the Straight Line tool and hold down the shift key as you make lines to divide the top rectangle into three days and the bottom one into four days. (See page 266 to see a sample schedule outline.)

3. Use Type Text from the GOODIES menu or the Typewriter tool to write the days of the week on your schedule.

4. Select the Rubber Stamps tool and choose the stamps that best represent your activities on each day of the week. Then place them on the appropriate days.

5. Use Type Text from the GOODIES menu or the Typewriter tool to write a title for you schedule.

What Else Can We Do: Now that you know how to make a weekly pictorial schedule, below are some of the ways you can put it to use.

1. You can make calendars showing what you did on your vacation and where you went.

2. You can print blank calendars and use them to keep track of your homework assignments. Staple them together to use them in book form.

3. You may want to make a copy of your schedule to put on the refrigerator at home, so your family knows what you will be doing from day to day.

My Weekly Schedule

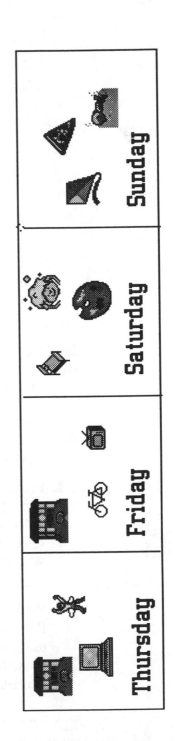

Holiday Acrostic

InfoNet: An acrostic is a verse or arrangement of words in which certain letters in each line, either at the beginning or end, when taken in order spell out a word.

This Project: You will be making your own acrostic, using the word "wreath." Almost any word will work for this project.

1. First you will need to write the word WREATH in capital letters down the left side of your screen. Select the Typewriter tool if you are using KPS, or select Type Text from the GOODIES menu in KP. Which ever program you are using, make sure you choose one of the fonts at the bottom of the screen.

2. Place the W at the upper left corner of the screen. Press the return or enter key once and the cursor will move to the correct position for the next letter. Type in the R and then repeat the rest of Step 2, until all of the letters are on the screen.

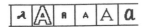

3. Select a smaller font to write a word that relates to a wreath and starts with the appropriate letter of the line you are on. Click the cursor after the next letter and write another word. Repeat this until there is a word after each letter.

4. Print your wreath. You may want to mount it on construction paper.

What Else Can We Do: Now that you have finished your first acrostic, you can make one for any occasion. Try some of the acrostics below, or come up with your own.

1. Try creating acrostics with other holiday words. An acrostic for Mother's Day would always be appreciated.

2. You can make acrostics using the names of countries or even you friends' names.

N orthern Country

O lympic Site Lillehammer '94

R ugged Mountains

W inter Wonderland

A lways Friendly People

Y outh Ski

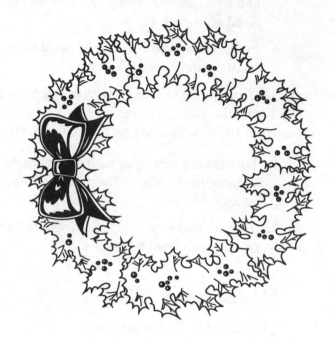

W elcoming

R ound

E verlasting

A rtistic

T hankful

H oliday

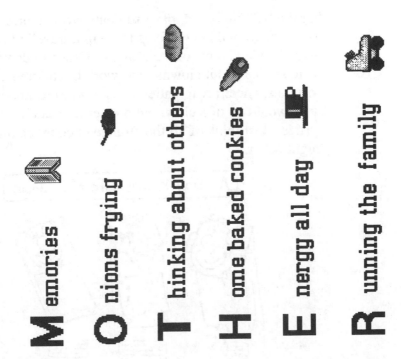

M emories

O nions frying

T hinking about others

H ome baked cookies

E nergy all day

R unning the family

Bulletin Board and Extension Ideas

The *Kid Pix* projects in this book lend themselves uniquely to classroom bulletin board displays. Displaying students' published works gives value to their endeavors. How excited parents will be during classroom visitations to see their children's computer work displayed.

Clowning Around

After students have made their puppets, have the clowns join the primary classes in their oral language arts activities. The clowns can help the students learn spelling words, tell stories, read to them, and dramatize classroom situations.

For the bulletin board, have students write stories about their clowns and how it feels to be in a traveling circus from the viewpoints of the clowns. Other students can write stories about clowns who work in children's hospitals, cheering up patients. A humorous approach to a story would be of a clown who entertains at children's parties. Just think of all the strange encounters that might occur.

Imitate Great Art

The teacher displays copies of the original artist's work and students display their interpretations. They also can research the life and times of their artist and report on what particular aspect of the artist's life contributed to his/her art work. In other words, what gave the artist his/her view of life as he/she portrays it. For example, explore the relationship of Picasso's moods to his artistic endeavors.

Life at the Seashore

Under the bulletin board provide a table on which students display their collections of sealife. Take a large piece of butcher paper and draw a line defining the seashore, the land, and below the waterline. Students research life at the various depths of the sea. Using *Kid Pix* students can draw specific sea animals and place them at the proper depth.

On the display table, an interesting method of display is to use a box filled with sand and place the seashells on the sand. Include books at various reading levels on the display table.

Morse Code

Have a student make a large print of the Morse code on a piece of tagboard or butcher paper. Attach a box to the bulletin board or place it on a table. Students write messages to their friends in Morse code and place them in the box for distribution.

This project lends itself well to expanding on the natural curiosity that students have regarding codes. Several books are available on codes at the intermediate grade level, and these would make a nice ancillary display. Perhaps a book on the life of Morse would spark interest in further research. A student could find out why the code was necessary and ways that it has been used throughout the years. This could lead your class to study the current use of codes in technology.

Family Quilts

Assemble the individual quilts, paste them onto a large piece of tagboard and display them on the bulletin board. The title of the board could be "Room Three's Families."

Quilts can be made for many different subjects. Health quilts could show the best foods to be eaten for optimum health and energy. Sports quilts could be made relating to the particular sports season (e.g., baseball, football, soccer, tennis, etc.).

As students think about their futures, they might construct a career quilt. These electronic quilts make excellent displays for parents to observe.

Assemble the quilts into a slide show. Save it as a self-running slide show and show it during Open House or Back to School Night.

Spanish Number Books

Make other books in the languages of your classroom. For homework, students can confer with their parents for the number names in their native languages.

Basic vocabulary books can be made in any language. They can include numbers, foods, animals, etc. Students pretend that they are traveling to another country, find the words that they will need in order to survive, and place them in a travel dictionary that they create with *Kid Pix*.

Fractions

Use yarn to construct a large pizza on the bulletin board and use yarn segments to divide the pizza into different fractions.

Students then illustrate the fraction you have shown in *Kid Pix* and write a fraction story.

Some students can write fraction stories, and others can use *Kid Pix* to illustrate the stories.

Rubber Stamps

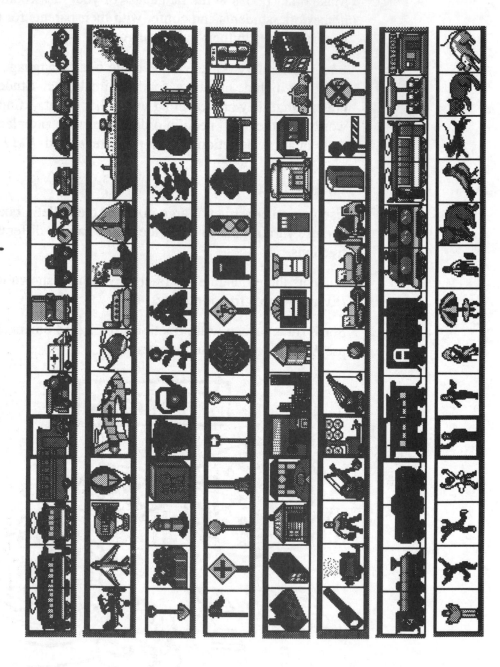

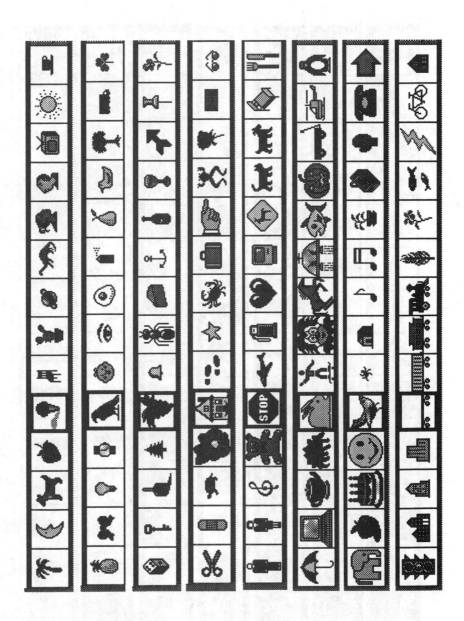

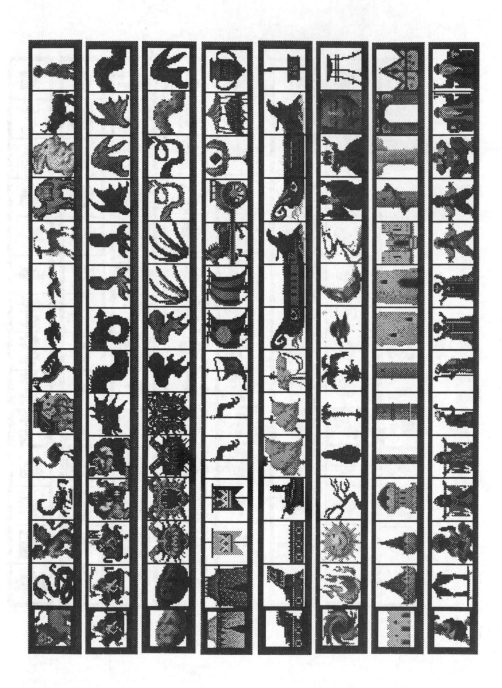

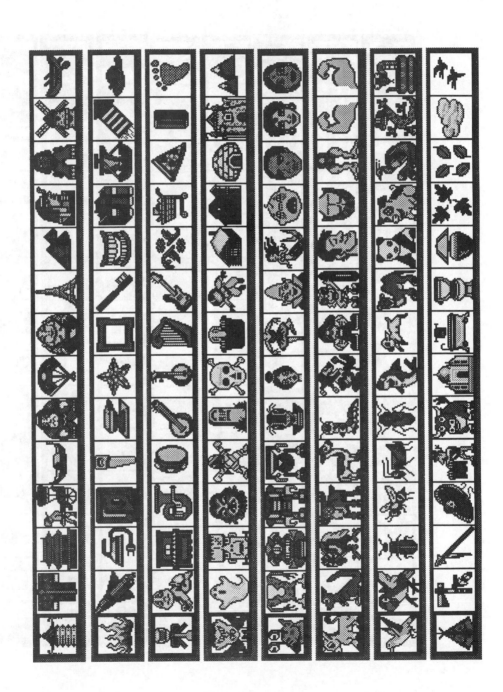

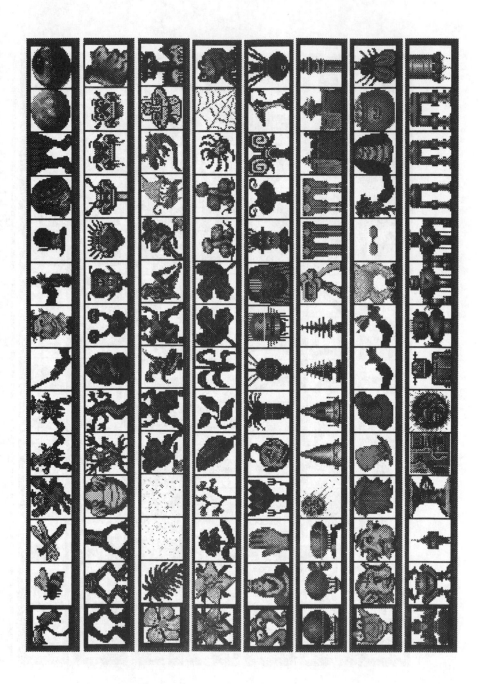

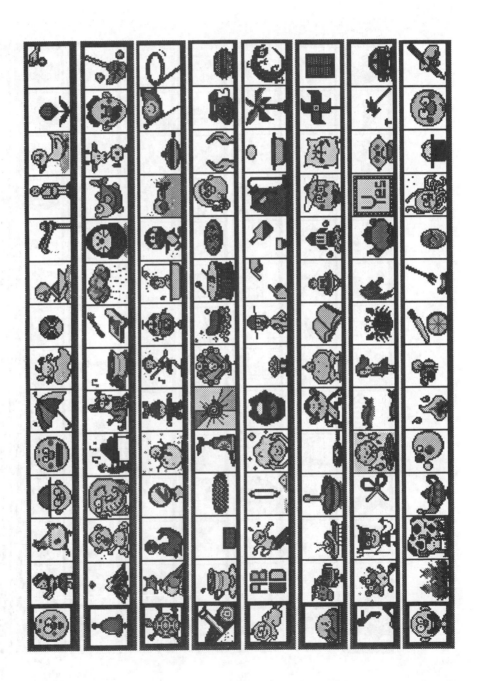

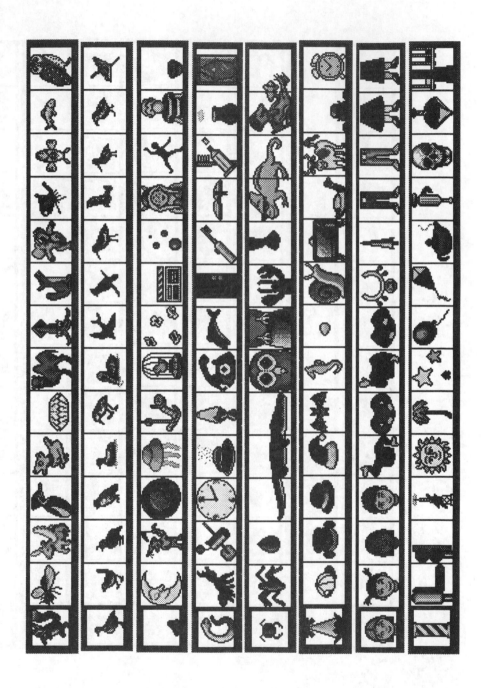

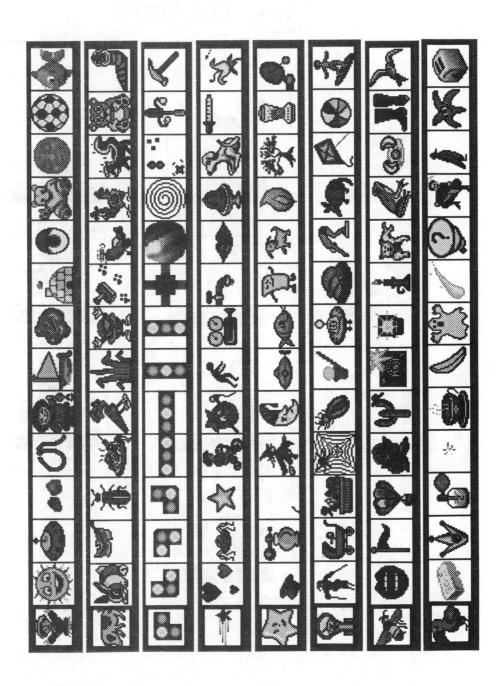

Digital Puppets

Alien

Albert

Rasta

Dragon

Dufus

Peteroo

Shelley

Nile princess

Garden Sal

Buster

Option Icons

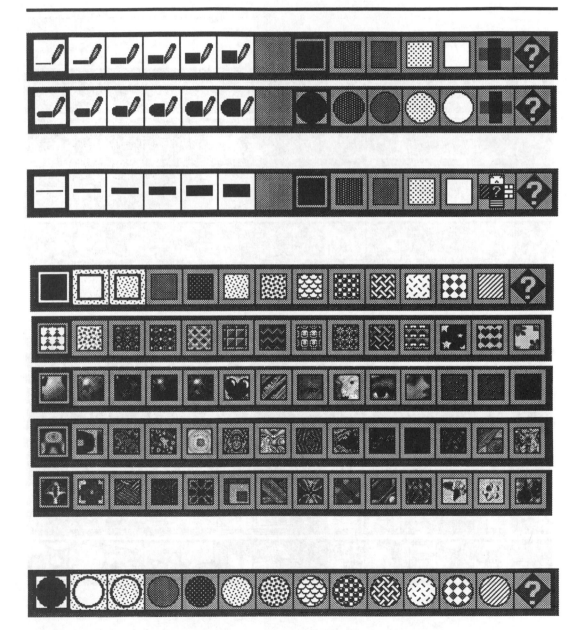

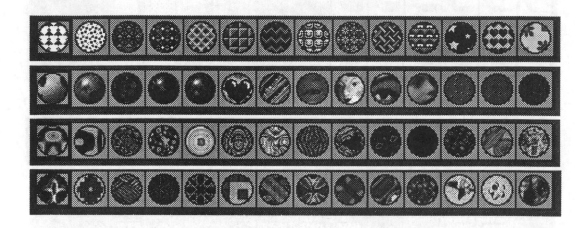

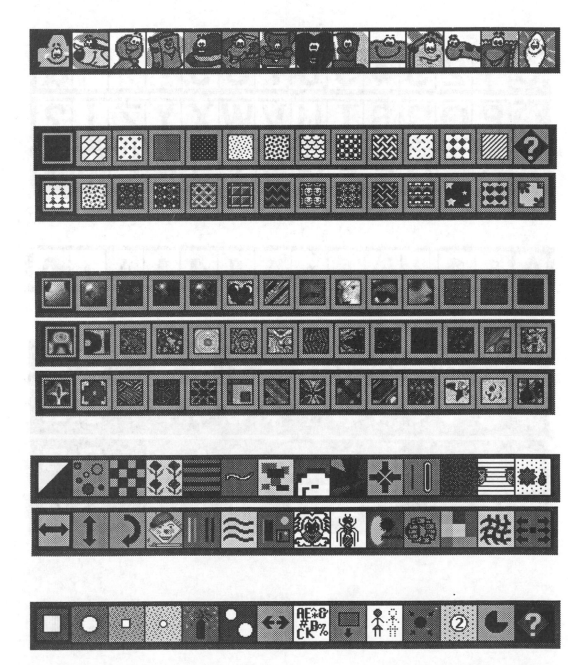

0 1 2 3 4 5 6 7 8 9 + - = &

O P Q R S T U V W X Y Z ! ?

A B C D E F G H I J K L M N

Grading Rubrics for Multimedia Presentations

	3	2	1	0
Overall Presentation	Project flows well, presentation is very interesting, and instructions were followed completely.	Project flows well, presentation is interesting, and instructions were mostly followed.	Project is disjointed, has low interest level, and most of the instructions were not followed.	No response.
Visual and/or Audio Presentation (graphics, laserdisc, scanned images, or sounds)	Uses a variety of images from several sources. Images used enhance the idea and topic of the project.	Uses one or more images from one or more sources, and images mostly enhance the idea and topic of the project.	Not enough images used and does not support or enhance project ideas or topic.	No response.
Use of Technology	Demonstrates total understanding of how technology is used for the project. Uses the technology in an appropriate manner in which to communicate ideas. Displays proper respect and appropriate behavior when using the technology.	Demonstrates some understanding of how the technology is used for the project. Displays proper respect and appropriate behavior when using the technology.	Shows no understanding of how the technology is used for the project. Displays proper respect and appropriate behavior when using the technology.	No response.

Job Performance Record

Name: _____

Project: _____

Keep track of the duties you perform in your group each day you work on your project. Have the other students in your group initial each day to verify that you fulfilled your responsibilities.

Day #: _____ Date: _____

Job: _____

The things I contributed to my group were

_____

_____

Students' Initials: _____

Day #: _____ Date: _____

Job: _____

The things I contributed to my group were

_____

_____

Students' Initials: _____

Day #: _____ Date: _____

Job: _____

The things I contributed to my group were

_____

_____

Student's Initials: _____

Day #: _____ Date: _____

Job: _____

The things I contributed to my group were

_____

_____

Students' Initials: _____

Project Assessment Form

Name _____

Date _____

This is how I felt about the project:_____

_____

_____

_____

	Yes	No
I followed directions.	_____	_____
I used the computer well.	_____	_____
I planned ahead.	_____	_____
I can help others with this project.	_____	_____

293

Student Self-Assessment for *Kid Pix*

Name: _____

Circle the number that tells how you did. The number five is the best.

1. I can use most of the *Kid Pix* tools.	1	2	3	4	5
2. I can save to a floppy disk.	1	2	3	4	5
3. I can use the text tool to write.	1	2	3	4	5
4. I can move an object on the screen.	1	2	3	4	5
5. I can add graphics, text, and sound.	1	2	3	4	5
6. I can create a slide show.	1	2	3	4	5
7. I can make a picture tell a story.	1	2	3	4	5
8. I can use a storyboard for creation.	1	2	3	4	5
9. I can use the mouse well.	1	2	3	4	5
10. I can change graphics.	1	2	3	4	5

This is what I like best about this program. _____

_____

Next time I would like to learn how to _____

_____

I think a fun project with *Kid Pix* would be to_____

_____

Student Self-Assessment for Individual Projects

Name: _____

1. In this project I learned how to _____

   _____

   _____

   _____

2. I thought that the best part of my project was_____

   _____

   _____

   _____

3. Next time I do this project, I want to _____

   _____

   _____

   _____

4. I used some of these tools and options in my project_____

   _____

   _____

   _____

5. I would like to learn how to do _____

   _____

   _____

   _____

6. Overall, I thought my project was:

   Good   Very Good   Great   Unbelievable

Kid Pix Storyboard

Name: _____ Date: _____

Slide # _____

Words/Narration: _____

_____

_____

_____

_____

_____

Slide # _____

Words/Narration: _____

_____

_____

_____

_____

_____

Slide # _____

Words/Narration: _____

_____

_____

_____

_____

_____

Slide # _____

Words/Narration: _____

_____

_____

_____

_____

_____

Glossary

Adapter—electronic piece that adapts to a device so a computer can control the device.

After Dark—a utility from Berkeley Systems called a screen saver.

AppleTalk—the AppleTalk network is how your Mac talks to your laser printer, other Macs, or other machines. All these machines need to be hooked up in order to talk.

Application—a computer software program you use.

Bar Code—grouping of thin lines which when accessed by an electronic bar-code reader, reveal information.

Baud (baud rate)—speed at which a modem can send information.

Bit—short for binary digit. One bit is the smallest unit of information that the computer can work with.

Bulletin Board Service—service usually set up by an online organization to provide or exchange information.

Bundling—usually, the practice of selling hardware (e.g., a computer) and including free one or more pieces of software.

Button—electronic item on a computer screen that is "pushed" in order for something to happen.

Byte—a byte is eight bits strung together. Most computer information is organized into bytes.

CD-ROM—compact disk read-only memory. A disk which holds up to 600 megabytes of information.

C

CD-ROM Player—disk drive which allows the CD-ROM to be played.

Clip Art—artwork that is electronically cut and pasted onto other documents.

CPU—central processing unit. The "brains" of a computer. Often a tiny microprocessor chip which runs the entire system.

Crash—what happens when your computer stops working suddenly or the system breaks down. (A very bad deal!)

Cursor—little mark indicating your position on the screen. It sometimes blinks on and off and will move when you move the mouse or press certain keys.

D

Database—collection of information stored in computerized form.

Default—any time an automatic decision is already made for you by the computer or software program.

Desktop—background on your screen when you are using a Macintosh or other windows-like program.

Desktop Publishing—process of creating printed documents that look professionally produced.

Dialog Box—a box or window on the screen that you can "dialog" with and make choices from.

Digital—information represented by numbers.

Digital Camera—outputs images in digital form instead of regular photographic film.

Disk—thin, circular, or rectangular object used to store computer data.

Disk Drive—part of the computer where the disk goes.

DOS—disk operating systems. Many types of computers have systems called DOS. Usually refers to IBM PC or other compatible computers.

Download—to receive information (like a file) from

D

another computer to yours through the modem. Or you may take a copy of a document from a disk and download it onto your computer.

Drag—use the mouse to position the pointer over an object, press and hold the mouse button and move the mouse, thereby moving the object to another position on the screen.

E

e-mail—short for electronic mail you can send or receive directly on your computer via modem.

Ethernet—a local area network connecting computers together with cables so the computers can share the same information.

F

Fiber Optics—a communications system that uses dozens of hair-thin strands of glass that move information at the speed of light.

Font—a complete set of type of one size and style.

G

Graphic—an electronic picture.

H

Hacker—computer enthusiast who is willing to "hack" away at understanding the computer for long periods of time.

Hardware—parts of the computer which are external (modem, printer, hard drive, keyboard).

HyperCard/HyperStudio—software applications which use multimedia and are interactive.

I

IBM (International Business Machines)—an international computer company.

Icons—little pictures on the screen which represent files of other computer applications.

Import—to bring information from one document or

I

computer screen into another document.

Interactive—program, game, or presentation where the user has some control over what is going on.

Interface—connection between two items so they can work together.

Internet—worldwide network of about half a million computers belonging to research organizations, the military, institutions of learning, corporations, and so on.

K, KB (Kilobyte)—a unit for measuring the size of things on hard disks or computer applications. It represents the memory of an item. One kilobyte is equal to 1,024 bytes.

Keyboard—piece of hardware that has keys like a typewriter.

L

Laptop Computer—a computer small enough to fit on your lap. Runs on batteries and is portable.

Laserdisc—also known as videodisc, similar to a music CD, but it also holds visual images. Information can be accessed by remote control or bar code.

Laserdisc Player—machine which plays the laserdisc.

Laser Printer—printer which produces documents that look professionally printed.

LCD Panel—a device which fits over the overhead projector and when connected to a computer will project whatever is on the computer screen onto a large viewing screen. LCD means liquid crystal display. A liquid compound is wedged between two grids of electrodes to create an image.

Macintosh—name of an Apple computer which was the first computer to use the windows and mouse formats.

Mb, MB (Megabyte)—short for a unit of measure

measuring the size of electronic items (like files and documents). One megabyte is equal to 1,048,567 bytes of memory.

Memory—temporary storage space in your computer as opposed to the permanent storage space on the hard disk. Think of the hard disk as a filing cabinet where everything is stored. Memory is your desk while you are temporarily working on the items inside the filing cabinet.

Menu—a displayed list of commands or options from which you can choose.

Modem—device that allows computers to communicate with other computers via the telephone line.

Monitor—another word for the computer screen.

Mouse—small device connected to the keyboard which you move across the top of your desk to manipulate the pointer or cursor on the screen.

Mouse Pad—a small pad on which you can roll your mouse around. Designed to give you a better grip than a desktop.

MS-DOS (Microsoft Disk Operating System)—this is the most commonly used system for IBM PCs and other compatible computers.

Multimedia—a computer presentation that involves still images, moving video, sound, animation, art, or a combination of all the above.

Network—communication or connection system that lets your computer talk with another computer, printer, hard disk, or other device.

Online—communicating with other computers through your modem or network.

Paint Program—software application that provides electronic versions of paintbrushes, paint cans, eraser, pencils, scissors, etc., in order to create illustrations.

PC (Personal Computer)—designed to be used by an individual person.

Port—a socket usually found on the back of hardware where a cable is connected.

PowerBook—Apple's laptop computer.

Printer—device that takes the text and images sent from the computer and presents them on paper.

Prompt—a symbol or question on the screen that "prompts" you to take action and tell the computer what to do next.

QuickTime—software product from Apple that is loaded onto your computer so you can run movies. It requires a great deal of space.

RAM (Random Access Memory)—electronic circuits in your computer which hold information. It is the temporary memory used while the computer is turned on. You will need to save any work you do onto a disk or a file on the hard drive. Otherwise, your work will be lost when the computer is shut off. RAM is referred to as volatile because the contents disappear when the computer is turned off.

ROM (Read-Only Memory)—information stored on ROM remains intact. The information is usually programmed right onto the chip or disk and cannot be altered or added to. That is why it is called read-only.

Scanner—device that takes a picture of an image that exists outside the computer and digitizes the image to put it on the computer.

S

Screen Saver—a software application that blanks the screen and replaces the screen with a nonharmful picture. By moving the mouse or touching a key, the screen saver shuts off, and your original screen automatically comes back up. If you leave your computer on for a long time, the image can burn onto the screen.

Software—instructions for the computer which are stored on a disk. These disks must be loaded onto the hard drive of the computer so that the computer will know what to do. Some software applications are already loaded onto the computer.

Spreadsheet Program—software program for financial or other number-related information processing. A spreadsheet is composed of rows and columns with individual boxes (cells) inside of each to hold information.

T

Telecommunications—communications carried on from one computer to another through the telephone line and modem.

Terminal—a screen and keyboard along with any circuits necessary to connect it to a main computer.

Toolbox—many software applications, especially ones with paint options, come with a toolbox which appears on the screen in the form of a palette.

U

Upgrade—to choose newer, more powerful packages (hard or software).

Upload—using a modem, you put one of your files onto a network (or online service) and load the file onto the service so other people have access to it.

U

Utility—a software program that is not used to create something (like an application) but rather it is used to enhance your working environment. *After Dark* is a utility for your computer system.

V

Videodisc—see laserdisc.

Virus—a software program designed to destroy data on your computer or corrupt your system software. Some viruses are so destructive, they can wipe out entire disks. Viruses are created illegally and can travel from computer to computer through disks, networks, and modems. Using virus detection software is a safe way to protect your system.

Virtual Reality—a simulated environment which appears to be real through use of a computer.

W

Window—rectangular frame on the screen in which you see and work with a particular software application.

Word Processor—software applications that allow you to type documents with a variety of tools to make work time easier and more efficient.